TORAH STUDIES

CHAIRMAN
Rabbi Moshe Kotlarsky

PRINCIPAL BENEFACTOR
Mr. George Rohr

EXECUTIVE DIRECTOR
Rabbi Efraim Mintz

TORAH STUDIES CHAIRMAN
Rabbi Yosef Gansburg

———

MANAGING EDITOR
Rabbi Ahrele Loschak

ADMINISTRATOR
Rabbi Shlomie Tenenbaum

(888) YOUR-JLI / (718) 221-6900
WWW.MYJLI.COM

SEASON TWO | YEAR 16 | BOOK 58

ב"ה

TORAH STUDIES

A WEEKLY JOURNEY INTO THE SOUL OF TORAH

STUDENT TEXTBOOK

THE ROHR JEWISH LEARNING INSTITUTE
gratefully acknowledges the pioneering support of

George and Pamela Rohr

Since its inception, the JLI has been a beneficiary of the vision, generosity, care, and concern of the Rohr family.

In the merit of the tens of thousands of hours of Torah study by JLI students worldwide, may they be blessed with health, *Yiddishe nachat* from all their loved ones, and extraordinary success in all their endeavors.

DEDICATED TO

Rabbi Shloimy &
Mirele Greenwald

cherished partners with JLI in bringing the light
of Torah to hundreds of communities around the
world.

In the merit of the Torah studied by thousands of
students worldwide, may they be blessed with good
health, happiness, *nachas* from their loved ones, and
success in all their endeavors.

לאורך ימים ושנים טובים

Contents

1.

Shemos

Is There a Case for Perfectionism?

A Time to Be Right, a Time to Do What's Right

Dedicated in loving memory of Ben Tzion Ze'ev Telushkin,
בן ציון זאב בן הרב ישראל יוסף ודבורה רחל,
marking his passing on 14 Tishrei, 5781.

*May the merit of the Torah study worldwide accompany his soul in the world
of everlasting life and be a source of blessings to his family with much health,
happiness, nachas, and success.*

PARSHA OVERVIEW

Shemos

The Children of Israel multiply in Egypt. Threatened by their growing numbers, Pharaoh enslaves them and orders the Hebrew midwives, Shifrah and Puah, to kill all male babies at birth. When they do not comply, he commands his people to cast the Hebrew babies into the Nile.

A child is born to Yocheved, the daughter of Levi, and her husband, Amram. This baby is placed in a basket on the river, while the baby's sister, Miriam, stands watch from afar. Pharaoh's daughter discovers the boy, raises him as her son, and names him Moses.

As a young man, Moses leaves the palace and discovers the hardship of his brethren. He sees an Egyptian beating a Hebrew, and kills the Egyptian. The next day, he sees two Jews fighting; when he admonishes them, they reveal his deed of the previous day, and Moses is forced to flee to Midian. There, he rescues Jethro's daughters, marries one of them (Tziporah), and becomes a shepherd of his father-in-law's flocks.

G-d appears to Moses in a burning bush at the foot of Mount Sinai and instructs him to go to Pharaoh and demand, "Let My people go, so that they may serve Me." Moses's brother, Aaron, is appointed to serve as his spokesman. In Egypt, Moses and Aaron assemble the elders of Israel to tell them that the time of their redemption has come. The people believe, but Pharaoh refuses to let them go and even intensifies the suffering of Israel.

Moses returns to G-d to protest, "Why have You done evil to this people?" G-d promises that their redemption is close at hand.

I. WHO'S YOUR PICK: MOSES OR ELIJAH?

Elijah: Perfectionism

TEXT 1

I MELACHIM (I KINGS) 18:21–22

וַיִּגַּשׁ אֵלִיָּהוּ אֶל כָּל הָעָם וַיֹּאמֶר, עַד מָתַי אַתֶּם פֹּסְחִים עַל שְׁתֵּי הַסְּעִפִּים? אִם ה' הָאֱלֹקִים לְכוּ אַחֲרָיו, וְאִם הַבַּעַל לְכוּ אַחֲרָיו. וְלֹא עָנוּ הָעָם אֹתוֹ דָּבָר:

וַיֹּאמֶר אֵלִיָּהוּ אֶל הָעָם, אֲנִי נוֹתַרְתִּי נָבִיא לַה' לְבַדִּי, וּנְבִיאֵי הַבַּעַל אַרְבַּע מֵאוֹת וַחֲמִשִּׁים אִישׁ:

And Elijah drew near to all the people and said, "Until when are you hopping between two ideas? If the L-rd is G-d, go after Him, and if the Baal, go after him." And the people did not answer him a word.

And Elijah spoke to the people, "I have remained a prophet to G-d by myself, and the prophets of the Baal are four hundred and fifty men."

TEXT **2**

I MELACHIM (I KINGS) 19:10

> וַיֹּאמֶר, קַנֹּא קִנֵּאתִי לַה' אֱלֹקֵי צְבָאוֹת, כִּי עָזְבוּ בְרִיתְךָ בְּנֵי יִשְׂרָאֵל, אֶת מִזְבְּחֹתֶיךָ הָרָסוּ וְאֶת נְבִיאֶיךָ הָרְגוּ בֶחָרֶב. וָאִוָּתֵר אֲנִי לְבַדִּי, וַיְבַקְשׁוּ אֶת נַפְשִׁי לְקַחְתָּהּ:

And he said, "I have been zealous for the L-rd, the G-d of Hosts, for the Children of Israel have forsaken Your covenant. They have torn down Your altars, and they have killed Your prophets by the sword, and I have remained alone, and they seek my life to take it."

TEXT **3**

MALACHI 3:23

> הִנֵּה אָנֹכִי שֹׁלֵחַ לָכֶם אֵת אֵלִיָּה הַנָּבִיא, לִפְנֵי בּוֹא יוֹם ה' הַגָּדוֹל וְהַנּוֹרָא:

Lo, I will send you Elijah the Prophet before the coming of the great and awesome day of G-d.

Moses: Work in Progress

TEXT 4

SHEMOT (EXODUS) 4:13

וַיֹּאמֶר בִּי אֲדֹנָי, שְׁלַח נָא בְּיַד תִּשְׁלָח:

But he said, "I beseech You, O G-d, send now [Your message] with whom You would send."

TEXT 5

MIDRASH PIRKEI RABBI ELIEZER, CH. 40

אמר לפניו: רבון כל העולמים "שלח נא ביד תשלח". רצה לומר, ביד
אותו האיש שאתה עתיד לשלוח. אמר לו: לא אמרתי "לך ואשלחך אל
ישראל", אלא "לך ואשלחך אל פרעה". ולאותו האיש שאתה אומר –
אני שולח לעתיד לבוא אל ישראל, שנאמר: "הנה אנכי שולח לכם את
אליהו הנביא".

Pirkei Rabbi Eliezer

A Midrash bearing the name of Rabbi Eliezer ben Hyrcanus, a prominent rabbinic sage living during the first and second centuries. *Pirkei Rabbi Eliezer* commences with the story of the early days of Rabbi Eliezer's life and then chronologically narrates and expounds upon events from the Creation until the middle of the journeys of the Children of Israel in the wilderness.

Moses said to G-d, "Send now [Your message] with whom You would send," namely, with the person You are planning on sending in the future.

G-d responded, "I did not say, 'Go and deliver the message to the *Jewish people*'; rather, 'Go and deliver the message to Pharaoh.' As for the person of whom you speak, I indeed plan on sending him in the future to the Jewish people, as the verse states, 'Lo, I will send you Elijah the prophet [before the coming of the great and awesome day of G-d].'"

II. IT'S GETTING BETTER

Adjusting the Spiritual Modeling?

TEXT 6

MIDRASH BEREISHIT RABAH, 14:7

רבי יהודה בר סימון אומר: . . . עולם על מליאתו נברא.

Rabbi Yehudah ben Simon said, "The world was created perfect and whole."

TEXT 7

ZOHAR 1, 52B

בשעתא דקיימו ישראל על טורא דסיני, אתעבר מנייהו זוהמא דהאי
חויא . . . הוו ידעין והוו חמאן אספקלריאן עלאין, ואתנהרן עינייהו . . .
דלא יכיל לשלטאה עלייהו האי חויא, ולא יסאב לון כבקדמיתא.

כיון דחטו בעגלא, אתעברו מנייהו כל אינון דרגין ונהורין עילאין . . .
ואמשיכו עלייהו חויא בישא כמלקדמין, וגרימו מותא לכל עלמא.

When the Jewish people stood at [Mount] Sinai, they were scrubbed of the snake's stain. . . . They were exposed to incredible visions of spiritual light, and their eyes were opened . . . in a way that the stain of the snake could not contaminate them, rendering them immune to history's earlier filth.

But when they sinned with the golden calf, all the spiritual light left them . . . and they were recontaminated with the snake's bite as earlier, bringing death to the entire world.

Bereishit Rabah

An early rabbinic commentary on the Book of Genesis. This Midrash bears the name of Rabbi Oshiya Rabah (Rabbi Oshiya "the Great"), whose teaching opens this work. This Midrash provides textual exegeses and stories, expounds upon the biblical narrative, and develops and illustrates moral principles. Produced by the sages of the Talmud in the Land of Israel, its use of Aramaic closely resembles that of the Jerusalem Talmud. It was first printed in Constantinople in 1512 together with 4 other Midrashic works on the other 4 books of the Pentateuch.

Zohar

The seminal work of kabbalah, Jewish mysticism. The *Zohar* is a mystical commentary on the Torah, written in Aramaic and Hebrew. According to the Arizal, the *Zohar* contains the teachings of Rabbi Shimon bar Yocha'i, who lived in the Land of Israel during the 2nd century. The *Zohar* has become one of the indispensable texts of traditional Judaism, alongside and nearly equal in stature to the Mishnah and Talmud.

The Spiritual Ladder of History

TEXT 8

THE REBBE, RABBI MENACHEM MENDEL SCHNEERSON, LIKUTEI SICHOT 11, P. 9

Rabbi Menachem Mendel Schneerson
1902–1994

The towering Jewish leader of the 20th century, known as "the Lubavitcher Rebbe," or simply as "the Rebbe." Born in southern Ukraine, the Rebbe escaped Nazi-occupied Europe, arriving in the U.S. in June 1941. The Rebbe inspired and guided the revival of traditional Judaism after the European devastation, impacting virtually every Jewish community the world over. The Rebbe often emphasized that the performance of just one additional good deed could usher in the era of Mashiach. The Rebbe's scholarly talks and writings have been printed in more than 200 volumes.

> והנה ידוע אשר "ירידה צורך עליה היא", והיינו שכל תכליתה של ירידה
> ממדריגה הקודמת היא לצורך עליה הבאה על ידה – הרי מובן שהעליה
> שלאחרי הירידה יש בה עליה לגבי העילוי שהיה קודם הירידה. ומובן
> מזה שמדריגת העליה על ידי מתן תורה שבאה לאחרי הירידה על ידי
> חטא עץ הדעת, יש בה יתרון על דרגת העילוי שקודם חטא עץ הדעת;
> ובודאי שכמו כן הוא ביתרון מעלתה של העליה העתידה (שלאחרי
> הירידה בחטא העגל) לגבי העליה דמתן תורה (שקודם חטא העגל).

The notion that "every low leads to an even greater high" is well known. It states that the entire purpose of falling off the previous level is for the heights that can be achieved thereby. It follows that the heights reached after the fall are greater even relative to the perch one was at prior to the fall.

It follows that the level reached after *Matan Torah* that, in turn, came after the sin with the Tree of Knowledge is greater even than the perch at which the world stood prior to the sin with the Tree of Knowledge. The same is true with the heights that we will reach with the future Redemption (that comes after the sin of the golden calf) relative to the perch at which the world stood at *Matan Torah* (prior to the sin of the golden calf).

Matan Torah

TEXT 9

THE REBBE, RABBI MENACHEM MENDEL SCHNEERSON, LIKUTEI SICHOT 11, P. 10

דאף על פי שעל ידי חטא העגל חזרה זוהמתן של ישראל, מכל מקום לא היתה זוהמא זו כמו קודם מתן תורה. דלפי שהבירור והעילוי ד"פסקה זוהמתן" במתן תורה היה בדרגא נעלית יותר מדרגת העילוי קודם חטא עץ הדעת, והיינו שפעולתו היתה פנימית וחודרת יותר, לכן גם בירידה שלאחרי זה עדיין ניכרת פעולתו.

Even though the sin of the golden calf recontaminated the Jewish people, it still was not at the same level of contamination as before *Matan Torah*. This is because the plateau to which the Jews arrived when the contamination was scrubbed by *Matan Torah* was higher than where the world stood prior to the sin of the Tree of Knowledge. In other words, the impact of *Matan Torah* was closer to home and with greater saturation, and so, even when the Jews thereafter fell, the residual impact was still felt.

Graduating to the Messianic Era

TEXT 10

MIDRASH SHEMOT RABAH, 29:9

> אמר רבי אבהו בשם רבי יוחנן: כשנתן הקדוש ברוך הוא את התורה,
> צפור לא צווח, עוף לא פרח, שור לא געה, אופנים לא עפו, שרפים
> לא אמרו קדוש קדוש, הים לא נזדעזע, הבריות לא דברו. אלא העולם
> שותק ומחריש, ויצא הקול "אנכי ה' אלוקיך".

Said Rabbi Abahu in the name of Rabbi Yochanan, "When the Holy One gave the Torah, no bird screeched, no fowl flew, no ox mooed, none of the *ophanim* [angels] flapped a wing, nor did the *seraphim* [burning celestial beings] chant '*Kadosh, Kadosh, Kadosh* [Holy, Holy, Holy!]*'* The sea did not roar, and none of the creatures uttered a sound. Throughout the entire world there was only a deafening silence, as the Divine Voice went forth speaking, "I am the L-rd your G-d."

Shemot Rabah

An early rabbinic commentary on the Book of Exodus. "Midrash" is the designation of a particular genre of rabbinic literature usually forming a running commentary on specific books of the Bible. *Shemot Rabah*, written mostly in Hebrew, provides textual exegeses, expounds upon the biblical narrative, and develops and illustrates moral principles. It was first printed in Constantinople in 1512 together with 4 other Midrashic works on the other 4 books of the Pentateuch.

TEXT 11

ZECHARIAH (ZACHARIAH) 13:2

> וְהָיָה בַיּוֹם הַהוּא, נְאֻם ה' צְבָאוֹת, אַכְרִית אֶת שְׁמוֹת הָעֲצַבִּים מִן הָאָרֶץ
> וְלֹא יִזָּכְרוּ עוֹד, וְגַם אֶת הַנְּבִיאִים וְאֶת רוּחַ הַטֻּמְאָה אַעֲבִיר מִן הָאָרֶץ:

And it shall come to pass on that day, says the L-rd of Hosts: I will cut off the names of the idols from the earth, and they shall no longer be mentioned. And also the prophets and the spirit of evil I will remove from the earth.

TEXT 12

RABBI SHALOM DOVBER SCHNEERSOHN, SEFER HAMAAMARIM 5643, P. 84

במתן תורה, הגם שהיה גילוי אלקות למטה, מכל מקום המטה היה במקומו – שלא נזדכך כלל, אלא הוא מטה כמו שהיה קודם.

ומה שבמתן תורה פסקה זוהמתן, אפשר לומר שהוא כמו שכתוב בספר של בינונים, בבינונים – שהרע שבהם ישן, ויכול להיות חוזר וניעור. כמו כן כאן – הרי אחר כך היה חטא העגל שחזרה זוהמתן, והרי זה שינוים, והיינו שגם מתחלה לא נזדכך לגמרי. ולעתיד לבוא יהיה מלמטה למעלה, פירוש – שהמטה יזדכך ויהיה במקום המעלה, והיינו שהמטה יהיה כלי לגילוי אור אין סוף.

Rabbi Shalom Dovber Schneersohn (Rashab) 1860–1920

Chasidic rebbe. Rabbi Shalom Dovber became the 5th leader of the Chabad movement upon the passing of his father, Rabbi Shmuel Schneersohn. He established the Lubavitch network of *yeshivot* called Tomchei Temimim. He authored many volumes of Chasidic discourses and is renowned for his lucid and thorough explanations of kabbalistic concepts.

While there was an intense G-dly revelation at *Matan Torah*, the world remained entrenched in its place, unrefined as it was prior.

How can we say this when the Talmud states that the world was scrubbed from its contamination?

We could suggest in similar fashion to what is explained in *Tanya* about the *benoni*, namely, that his negative urges are "asleep"—but always ready to and able to be awakened. So it is here: After *Matan Torah*, the Jews sinned with the golden calf and were recontaminated. This is because they were never **entirely refined.**

In the future Redemption, by contrast, the world will be completely transformed, vaulted to a lofty perch. In other words, the world will be transformed into a vehicle for the highest levels of G-dliness.

III. THE ROAD TO PERFECTION RUNS THROUGH IMPERFECTION

The Characters Involved—Moses and Mashiach

TEXT 13

BEREISHIT (GENESIS) 49:10

לֹא יָסוּר שֵׁבֶט מִיהוּדָה וּמְחֹקֵק מִבֵּין רַגְלָיו, עַד כִּי יָבֹא שִׁילֹה, וְלוֹ יִקְּהַת עַמִּים:

The scepter shall not depart from Judah, nor the student of the law from between his feet, until Shiloh comes, and to him will be a gathering of peoples.

Moses and Elijah

TEXT 14

THE REBBE, RABBI MENACHEM MENDEL SCHNEERSON,
LIKUTEI SICHOT 11, P. 12, AND FOOTNOTE 50

ענינו של מתן תורה שהוא ענינו של משה . . . הרי הוא נתינת הכח על
העבודה בבירור וזיכוך העולם; ענינו של משיח הוא גמר הבירור והזיכוך
והעיקר העבודה לאחרי זה, כאשר העולם כבר יתברר ויזדכך וכו'.

ויש לומר, שזהו גם תוכן מענה הקדוש ברוך הוא למשה: לא אמרתי לך
"לך ואשלחך אל ישראל", אלא "לך ואשלחך אל פרעה", לאותו איש
שאתה אומר, אני שולח לעתיד לבוא אל ישראל כו'.

כי ענינו של משה הוא בעוד שיש מציאות "פרעה" בעולם, לבררו
ולזככו כו', מה שאין כן ענינו של אליהו (ומשיח) הוא בעיקר לאחר
ש"ואת רוח הטומאה אעביר מן הארץ", כבפנים.

Moses's primary accomplishment was the events at *Matan Torah*, and he thereby empowered future generations to work on transforming the world. Mashiach's mission is to complete the transformation and bring about a time when all work will be in an environment of a perfect world.

This, then, is the significance of G-d's response to Moses, "l did not say, 'Go and deliver the message to the *Jewish people*'; rather, 'Go and deliver the message to *Pharaoh*.' As for the person of whom you speak, l indeed plan on sending him in the future to the Jewish people": Moses was about working in a world that has a Pharaoh, working hard to transform and refine it. By contrast, Elijah and Mashiach are primarily conditioned to operate in a world in which the "spirit of evil has been removed from the earth."

2.

Va'era

Line in the Sand

Sometimes, We Must Be Unequivocal

Dedicated to Rabbi Peretz Greenwald on the occasion of his birthday on 20 Teves.

May he go from strength to strength and enjoy good health, happiness, nachas from his loved ones, and success in all of his endeavors.

PARSHA OVERVIEW

Va'era

G-d reveals Himself to Moses. Employing the "four expressions of redemption," He promises to take out the Children of Israel from Egypt, deliver them from their enslavement, redeem them, and acquire them as His own chosen people at Mount Sinai; He will then bring them to the land He promised to the Patriarchs as their eternal heritage.

Moses and Aaron repeatedly come before Pharaoh to demand in the name of G-d, "Let My people go, so that they may serve Me in the wilderness." Pharaoh repeatedly refuses. Aaron's staff turns into a snake and swallows the magic sticks of the Egyptian sorcerers. G-d then sends a series of plagues upon the Egyptians.

The waters of the Nile turn to blood; swarms of frogs overrun the land; lice infest all men and beasts. Hordes of wild animals invade the cities; a pestilence kills the domestic animals; painful boils afflict the Egyptians. For the seventh plague, fire and ice combine to descend from the skies as a devastating hail. Still, "the heart of Pharaoh was hardened and he would not let the Children of Israel go, as G-d had said to Moses."

I. WHO WERE THE PLAGUES FOR?

A Discriminating Plague

TEXT 1

SHEMOT (EXODUS) 8:18

וְהִפְלֵיתִי בַיּוֹם הַהוּא אֶת אֶרֶץ גֹּשֶׁן אֲשֶׁר עַמִּי עֹמֵד עָלֶיהָ, לְבִלְתִּי הֱיוֹת
שָׁם עָרֹב, לְמַעַן תֵּדַע כִּי אֲנִי ה' בְּקֶרֶב הָאָרֶץ:

And I will separate on that day the land of Goshen, upon which My people stand; there will be no mixture of noxious creatures there, in order that you know that I am G-d in the midst of the earth.

TEXT 2

RABBI AVRAHAM IBN EZRA, SHEMOT (EXODUS) 7:24

> "ויחפרו": רבים אומרים כי המים היו ביד המצרי אדומים כדם ונתלבנו
> ביד הישראלי. אם כן, למה לא נכתב אות זה בתורה?
>
> ולפי דעתי, כי מכת הדם והצפרדעים והכינים – היתה כוללת המצרים
> והעבריים, כי אחר הכתוב נרדוף. ואלה השלש מעט הזיקו, רק מכת
> הערוב, שהיתה קשה, השם הפריש בין המצריים ובין ישראל.

Rabbi Avraham ibn Ezra
1092–1167

Biblical commentator, linguist, and poet. Ibn Ezra was born in Toledo, Spain, and fled the Almohad regime to other parts of Europe. It is believed that he was living in London at the time of his death. Ibn Ezra is best known for his literalistic commentary on the Pentateuch. He also wrote works of poetry, philosophy, medicine, astronomy, and other topics.

"And they dug." Many have said that water that was red like blood when in the hand of an Egyptian became clear in the hand of a Hebrew. If that is so, why is this miracle not recorded in the Torah?

In my view, following from the [simple meaning] of the Scriptures, the plagues of blood, frogs, and lice included the Egyptians and the Hebrews. These three plagues did not cause much harm; only for the plague of the wild animals, which was more destructive, [and subsequent plagues] did G-d distinguish between the Egyptians and Israel.

Why Is This Plague Different?

TEXT **3**

RABBEINU BECHAYE, SHEMOT (EXODUS) 8:18

"וְהִפְלֵיתִי בַיּוֹם הַהוּא": המכות הראשונות היו עומדות, אין מן הפלא
כל כך אם היו בארץ מצרים ולא בארץ גושן. אבל מכת הערוב – מכה
משולחת, וכאשר יבוא מן המדבר בגזירת הא-ל לעקור את הכל, היה
ראוי אף בדרך הטבע שיבואו גם בארץ גושן, כי היא מכלל ארץ מצרים.
אלא שהקדוש ברוך הוא הפלה ביניהם בדרך הנס.

**Rabbi Bachya ben
Asher Ibn Halawa
(Rabbeinu Bechaye)**
c. 1255–1340

Biblical commentator. Rabbeinu
Bechaye lived in Spain and was a
disciple of Rabbi Shlomo ben Aderet,
known as Rashba. He is best known
for his multifaceted commentary on
the Torah, which interprets the text
on literal, Midrashic, philosophical,
and kabbalistic levels. Rabbeinu
Bechaye also wrote *Kad Hakemach*,
a work on philosophy and ethics.

"And I will separate on that day." Inasmuch as the first plagues
were relatively stationary, it was unremarkable that they oc-
curred in the central part of Egypt, and not in Goshen [where the
Jews lived]. By contrast, wild animals wreak havoc everywhere.
When [these beasts] came on G-d's command from the desert
to destroy everything, it's only natural that they would reach
Goshen as well—since it was also part of the land of Egypt. The
Jews were only spared because of a miracle from G-d.

TEXT 4

RABBI DAVID IBN ZIMRA, RESPONSA RADBAZ, VOL. 1, §813

ומה שכתב הרב אבן עזרא, כי מכת הדם והצפרדעים וכינים היה
למצרים ולישראל – אסור להאמין דבר זה. כל שכן שהכתובים מורים
היפך: "ולא יכלו מצרים לשתות מים מן היאור", "ויחפרו כל מצרים
סביבות היאור", משמע, אבל ישראל לא היו צריכים לזה, כי היו שותים
ממימי היאור! ובצפרדעים כתיב: "ובכה ובעמך וגו'", "וסרו הצפרדעים
ממך ומבתיך ומעבדיך ומעמך וגו'", משמע שלא היו בישראל! וכן
הכינים, וילמוד סתום מן המפורש. ולא ידעתי, אם המכה היתה גם
לישראל – מה ראיה יש בה לפרעה שישלח את ישראל מארצו? ולא
היה ראוי להטריח הקולמוס בכיוצא בזה, אלא שלא ליתן פתחון פה
לדוברים עתק על דרשות רבותינו זכרונם לברכה.

Rabbi David ibn Zimra (Radbaz)
1479–1573

Noted halachist. Radbaz was born in Spain and immigrated to Safed, Israel, upon the expulsion of the Jews from Spain in 1492. In 1513, he moved to Egypt and served as rabbi, judge, and head of the yeshiva in Cairo. He also ran many successful business ventures and was independently wealthy. In 1553, he returned to Safed where he would later be buried. He authored what would later become a classic commentary to Maimonides's code of law and wrote many halachic responsa, of which more than 10,000 are extant.

Rabbi Avraham ibn Ezra writes that Egypt and Israel were both subject to the plagues of blood, frogs, and lice. It's forbidden to believe such a thing, especially since Scripture itself indicates the opposite: "And Egypt could not drink water from the river," and "All of Egypt dug around the river," the implication being that the Israelites did not need to do this, since they were drinking from the river's waters.

And so it is said [when Moses warned] of the frogs, that they will [come up] "into you and into your people," and then later that "they will depart from you, and from your houses, and from your servants, and from your people." Implied is that they were not in Israel. The same is true of the lice; from where it is clear, we can infer to where it is not clear.

I fail to understand: If the plague was also on Israel, then what proof did it hold for Pharaoh that he should send the Israelites from his land?

I shouldn't have bothered wasting ink on this sort of thing, but I did not want to give any space to those who speak falsely regarding the words of our sages.

TEXT 5

MAIMONIDES, PIRKEI AVOT (ETHICS OF THE FATHERS) 5:3

ולשון התורה בכל מכה ומכה מהן – שהביא הקדוש ברוך הוא על
המצריים בלבד. מלבד מכת הכינים שלא ביאר זה, אלא שהוא ידוע
שלא ענש ישראל. אבל היו נמצאים אצלם, ולא היו מצערים אותם.

**Rabbi Moshe ben Maimon
(Maimonides, Rambam)
1135–1204**

Halachist, philosopher, author, and physician. Maimonides was born in Córdoba, Spain. After the conquest of Córdoba by the Almohads, he fled Spain and eventually settled in Cairo, Egypt. There, he became the leader of the Jewish community and served as court physician to the vizier of Egypt. He is most noted for authoring the *Mishneh Torah*, an encyclopedic arrangement of Jewish law; and for his philosophical work, *Guide for the Perplexed*. His rulings on Jewish law are integral to the formation of halachic consensus.

For every plague that G-d brought upon the Egyptians, the Torah's language indicates that it was on the *Egyptians*—except for the plague of lice. While it is not stated explicitly, it is known that [the lice] did affect the Jews, but not as a punishment. And so it did not actually cause any suffering.

Did the plague afflict the Hebrews?	Ibn Ezra	Radbaz	Rambam
1. Blood	✓	x	x
2. Frogs	✓	x	x
3. Lice	✓	x	Somewhat
4. Wild animals	x	x	x
5. Animals dying	x	x	x
6. Boils	x	x	x
7. Hail	x	x	x
8. Locust	x	x	x
9. Darkness	x	x	x
10. Death of Firstborns	x	x	x

TEXT 6

RABBI YAAKOV YOSEF OF POLONYE, TOLEDOT YAAKOV YOSEF, BESHALACH 53

> שמעתי בשם מורי: עשר מכות לפרעה, כי השכחה הנקראת "פרעה"...
> וכן צפ"ר דע"ה, כי "צפר" לשון צפרא נהיר, ו"דעה" הוא היפוך השכחה
> הנקראת "פרעה". וכך היה זה מכה לפרעה, מה שאין כן לישראל היה
> צפ"ר דע"ה, והבן, ודברי פי חכם חן.

Rabbi Yaakov Yosef of Polonye
c. 1710–1784

Chasidic pioneer and author. Rabbi Yaakov Yosef was a dedicated disciple of the Baal Shem Tov, the founder of the Chasidic movement, and is credited with taking a leading role in the dissemination of the philosophy of Chasidism in its nascent years. He authored *Toledot Yaakov Yosef*, the first printed work of Chasidic philosophy. This work is cherished in Chasidic circles.

I heard in the name of my teacher that the Ten Plagues were directed at Pharaoh specifically, for Pharaoh is associated with forgetfulness [of spirituality]. . . . For example, the plague of *tzefarde'ah* [the plague of frogs]: The root-word *tzafar* [indicates light, as in the Aramaic for "a bright morning,"] *tzafra nahir*. *De'ah* [meaning knowledge] is the opposite of forgetfulness, which is called Pharaoh. Thus, it came as a plague to Pharaoh, but for Israel it was *tzafar-de'ah*.

Understand this, and there is charm in the words of the wise.

II. WHAT WERE THE PLAGUES FOR?

The Purpose of the Plagues

TEXT 7

SHEMOT (EXODUS) 8:17

כִּי אִם אֵינְךָ מְשַׁלֵּחַ אֶת עַמִּי, הִנְנִי מַשְׁלִיחַ בְּךָ וּבַעֲבָדֶיךָ וּבְעַמְּךָ וּבְבָתֶּיךָ אֶת הֶעָרֹב, וּמָלְאוּ בָּתֵּי מִצְרַיִם אֶת הֶעָרֹב, וְגַם הָאֲדָמָה אֲשֶׁר הֵם עָלֶיהָ:

For if you do not let My people go, behold, I will incite against you and against your servants and against your people and in your houses a mixture of noxious creatures, and the houses of Egypt will be filled with the mixture of noxious creatures, as well as the land upon which they are.

TEXT 8

BEREISHIT (GENESIS) 15:13–14

וַיֹּאמֶר לְאַבְרָם, יָדֹעַ תֵּדַע כִּי גֵר יִהְיֶה זַרְעֲךָ בְּאֶרֶץ לֹא לָהֶם, וַעֲבָדוּם וְעִנּוּ אֹתָם אַרְבַּע מֵאוֹת שָׁנָה:

וְגַם אֶת הַגּוֹי אֲשֶׁר יַעֲבֹדוּ דָּן אָנֹכִי, וְאַחֲרֵי כֵן יֵצְאוּ בִּרְכֻשׁ גָּדוֹל:

And G-d said to Abram, "You shall surely know that your seed will be strangers in a land that is not theirs, and they will enslave them and oppress them, for four hundred years.

"And also the nation that they will serve will I judge, and afterward they will go forth with great possessions."

TEXT 9

SHEMOT (EXODUS) 7:17

כֹּה אָמַר ה', בְּזֹאת תֵּדַע כִּי אֲנִי ה', הִנֵּה אָנֹכִי מַכֶּה בַּמַּטֶּה אֲשֶׁר בְּיָדִי עַל הַמַּיִם אֲשֶׁר בַּיְאֹר, וְנֶהֶפְכוּ לְדָם:

So said G-d, "With this you will know that I am the L-rd." Behold, I will smite with the staff that is in my hand upon the water that is in the Nile, and it will turn to blood.

The First Three Plagues—a State of De-Nile

TEXT 10a

RASHI, SHEMOT (EXODUS) 7:17

הלקה את יראתם, ואחר כך הלקה אותם.

He struck their deity, then He struck them.

Rabbi Shlomo Yitzchaki (Rashi)
1040–1105

Most noted biblical and Talmudic commentator. Born in Troyes, France, Rashi studied in the famed *yeshivot* of Mainz and Worms. His commentaries on the Pentateuch and the Talmud, which focus on the straightforward meaning of the text, appear in virtually every edition of the Talmud and Bible.

TEXT 10b

SHEMOT (EXODUS) 8:15

וַיֹּאמְרוּ הַחַרְטֻמִּם אֶל פַּרְעֹה, אֶצְבַּע אֱלֹקִים הִיא. וַיֶּחֱזַק לֵב פַּרְעֹה וְלֹא שָׁמַע אֲלֵהֶם, כַּאֲשֶׁר דִּבֶּר ה':

So the necromancers said to Pharaoh, "It is the finger of G-d," but Pharaoh's heart remained steadfast, and he did not hearken to them, as G-d had spoken.

A Universal Message

TEXT 11

THE REBBE, RABBI MENACHEM MENDEL SCHNEERSON, LIKUTEI SICHOT 11, P. 32

אולם על פי הנזכר לעיל מובן: מכיון שאת שתי המכות הראשונות,
פירש רש"י שהביא הקדוש ברוך הוא בשביל להלקות יראתם . . .
מטעם זה עצמו היה מוכרח שתהיינה ב' מכות אלו גם במים כו' של בני
ישראל, כי מכיון שעל ידי זה הלקה יראתם, הנה בכל מקום שנמצאת
יראתם היתה צריכה להיות המכה שם, דאם לא כן, יחשוב פרעה
שחלק זה מהעבודה זרה שלו (הנמצא בגושן וכיוצא בזה) גדול יותר,
חס ושלום, מהקדוש ברוך הוא.

Rabbi Menachem Mendel Schneerson
1902–1994

The towering Jewish leader of the 20th century, known as "the Lubavitcher Rebbe," or simply as "the Rebbe." Born in southern Ukraine, the Rebbe escaped Nazi-occupied Europe, arriving in the U.S. in June 1941. The Rebbe inspired and guided the revival of traditional Judaism after the European devastation, impacting virtually every Jewish community the world over. The Rebbe often emphasized that the performance of just one additional good deed could usher in the era of Mashiach. The Rebbe's scholarly talks and writings have been printed in more than 200 volumes.

Based on the above, we can understand: As Rashi explains, G-d brought the first two plagues to "strike their deity." . . . For this reason, the first two plagues had to also affect the Israelites' water: Inasmuch as "their deity" was being struck by the plagues, the plagues had to be wherever their deity was to be found. If not, Pharaoh could have thought that this particular section of his deity (the part in the Hebrew territory of Goshen) was indeed greater than the Holy One, Blessed be He, Heaven forfend.

III. THREE LESSONS

1. Lo Pelug—*We Do Not Differentiate*

TEXT 12

MAIMONIDES, TESHUVOT HARAMBAM (PE'ER HADOR) §145

יורינו מורינו, בחברת בני אדם התפללו ורובם בקיאים בתפילה – אם
יסדיר השליח ציבור עליהם, כדי שלא לבייש את מי שאינו בקי, מפני
שסידור התפילה נתקן על זה; או לא יסדר, מפני שהיא ברכה שאינה
צריכה, שהרי כבר יצאו ידי חובתן בלחש; או ירד שליח ציבור להתפלל,
ולא יתפללו לעצמן בלחש, כדי שלא תתבטל קדושת הסדרא . . .

תשובה: מאחר שתיקנו חכמינו זכרונם לברכה לחזור שליח ציבור לפני
התיבה להוציא מי שאינו בקי . . . לא תהיה חזרת שליח צבור ברכה
לבטלה בשום פנים בסיבת עיקר התקנה, עם היות שלא יש באלו
הקהל מי שלא יצא . . .

וכן כל מה שתיקנו בסיבת איזה סיבה, אין ענינו עד שתהיה שם אותה
הסיבה אשר מצידה נתקן, אבל ענינו שיעשה זה על כל פנים, גזירה
שמא תהיה שם הסיבה שנתקנה בשבילה. וראוי לשמור זה הענין, כי
לולי זה, היו חכמים זכרונם לברכה נותנין דבריהם לשיעורין, והיה ראוי
לראות כל אחד בבית הכנסת אם יש שם מי שאינו יודע, כדי לחזור
שליח ציבור התפילה בעדו, וזה כולו חוץ מענין התקנות והגזירות.

Question: What is the law with regard to a group of people
who are largely proficient in prayer? Should the *chazan* repeat
the Amidah so as not to embarrass those who aren't proficient,
as per the original edict, or perhaps he should not, so as to
refrain from uttering a blessing in vain? After all, most people
already discharged their obligation during the silent Amidah.
Or perhaps the congregants shouldn't pray at all on their own
and leave it to the *chazan* instead so as not to do away with the
established, sacred tradition? . . .

Answer: Inasmuch as our sages instituted that the *chazan* should repeat the Amidah for those who are not proficient . . . the *chazan*'s repetition is certainly not a blessing in vain, even if there aren't any people in the crowd who did not already discharge their obligation. . . .

This is how we ought to look at any rabbinic edict enacted for whatever reason: The edict is not in place only for as long as the reason still stands. Rather, the edict is now in force forever in the event that the reason comes up. This means that we ought to follow the edict regardless, for if not, the sages' words would be limited in context. We would then be compelled to look in each synagogue for a person who is not proficient in the prayer so the *chazan* can then repeat the Amidah for him. Such behavior is obviously not what an edict is all about.

Question for Discussion

What principle do you hold, but struggle to live up to?

The Upside of Obstinacy

TEXT **13**

MIDRASH SHEMOT RABAH, 42:9

> אָמַר רַבִּי יִצְחָק בַּר רַדִיפָא בְּשֵׁם רַבִּי אַמֵי: אַתָּה סָבוּר שֶׁהוּא לִגְנַאי, וְאֵינוֹ
> אֶלָּא לְשִׁבְחָן, אוֹ יְהוּדִי אוֹ צָלוּב.

Said Rabbi Ami, "When the Jewish people are described as stubborn, people normally understand this as a criticism, but in fact it is a compliment. [It is due to our stubbornness that] we have been willing to be killed for our Judaism."

Shemot Rabah

An early rabbinic commentary on the Book of Exodus. "Midrash" is the designation of a particular genre of rabbinic literature usually forming a running commentary on specific books of the Bible. *Shemot Rabah*, written mostly in Hebrew, provides textual exegeses, expounds upon the biblical narrative, and develops and illustrates moral principles. It was first printed in Constantinople in 1512 together with 4 other Midrashic works on the other 4 books of the Pentateuch.

TEXT **14**

RABBI YOSEF CARO, SHULCHAN ARUCH 155:1

> אחר שיצא מבית הכנסת, ילך לבית המדרש ויקבע עת ללמוד. וצריך
> שאותו עת יהיה קבוע, שלא יעבירנו, אף אם הוא סבור להרויח הרבה.

One should have a set time to learn Torah. The set time to learn Torah should not be altered even to allow for a large increase in revenue.

Rabbi Yosef Caro (Maran, *Beit Yosef*) 1488–1575

Halachic authority and author. Rabbi Caro was born in Spain but was forced to flee during the Expulsion in 1492 and eventually settled in Safed, Israel. He authored many works, including the *Beit Yosef, Kesef Mishneh*, and a mystical work, *Magid Meisharim*. Rabbi Caro's magnum opus, the Shulchan Aruch (Code of Jewish Law), has been universally accepted as the basis for modern Jewish law.

TEXT 15

RABBI YOSEF YITZCHAK SCHNEERSOHN, SEFER HAMAAMARIM 5710, P. 118

דישנם כמה דברים באדם שהוא נוהג ועושה כן וויילע אזוי טוט וועלט,
והדברים האלה הם כמו חוק שבלתי מזיזים אותו ממקומו, לפי דכן
הוא הנהגת העולם, וכמו בכמה עניני נימוס והדומה כו' – הנה את זה
צריכים להפכו אל הלמעלה מן הדעת בעבודה, וכמו על דרך משל זמני
האכילה וזמני השינה, הנה מצד הרגש העולם הם קבועים בעתים
וזמנים, וגם כשצריך להתעסק במשא ומתן, ומכל מקום, הנה זמנים
אלו על פי הרוב בלתי ניזזים ובלתי נידחים כלל ועיקר. וזמני הקביעות
של תורה ותפילה הם נידחים ואין להם קבע, ויש שהם נידחים חס
ושלום לגמרי. הנה האדם אשר נותן איזה חשבון לנפשו, האם יש איזה
חכמה בהנהגה כזו, דמי הוא היודע עיתו וזמנו.

Rabbi Yosef Yitzchak Schneersohn (Rayatz, Frierdiker Rebbe, Previous Rebbe) 1880–1950

Chasidic rebbe, prolific writer, and Jewish activist. Rabbi Yosef Yitzchak, the sixth leader of the Chabad movement, actively promoted Jewish religious practice in Soviet Russia and was arrested for these activities. After his release from prison and exile, he settled in Warsaw, Poland, from where he fled Nazi occupation and arrived in New York in 1940. Settling in Brooklyn, Rabbi Schneersohn worked to revitalize American Jewish life. His son-in-law Rabbi Menachem Mendel Schneerson succeeded him as the leader of the Chabad movement.

There are things that people do only because everyone does them. For example, certain cultural norms are conventionally considered "proper," and are then crystallized into unalterable laws.

Such unreasonable habits ought to be transformed through one's own endeavors: instead of remaining below reason, they should be elevated above reason.

Business commitments, for example, pressing as they may be, do not generally overrule the times that convention prescribes for eating and sleeping. They do, alas, sometimes set aside (or even cancel) the fixed times that should be regularly scheduled for Torah study and prayer.

A man who feels accountable to his soul should ask himself: "Is there any wisdom in such conduct?" For who is the man who knows when his time will come?

Avoid the Middle Ground

TEXT 16

MAIMONIDES, MISHNEH TORAH, LAWS OF CHARACTER 2:3

וְיֵשׁ דֵּעוֹת שֶׁאָסוּר לוֹ לָאָדָם לִנְהֹג בָּהֶן בְּבֵינוֹנִיּוּת, אֶלָּא יִתְרַחֵק מִן הַקָּצֶה
הָאֶחָד עַד הַקָּצֶה הָאַחֵר. וְהוּא: גֹּבַהּ לֵב. שֶׁאֵין דֶּרֶךְ הַטּוֹבָה שֶׁיִּהְיֶה אָדָם
עָנָו בִּלְבַד, אֶלָּא שֶׁיִּהְיֶה שְׁפַל רוּחַ וְתִהְיֶה רוּחוֹ נְמוּכָה לִמְאֹד. וּלְפִיכָךְ נֶאֱמַר
בְּמֹשֶׁה רַבֵּנוּ: "עָנָו מְאֹד" וְלֹא נֶאֱמַר "עָנָו" בִּלְבַד. וּלְפִיכָךְ צִוּוּ חֲכָמִים:
מְאֹד מְאֹד הֱוֵי שְׁפַל רוּחַ. וְעוֹד אָמְרוּ: שֶׁכָּל הַמַּגְבִּיהַּ לִבּוֹ כָּפַר בָּעִקָּר,
שֶׁנֶּאֱמַר: "וְרָם לְבָבֶךָ וְשָׁכַחְתָּ אֶת ה' אֱלֹקֶיךָ". וְעוֹד אָמְרוּ: בְּשַׁמְתָּא מַאן
דְּאִית בֵּיהּ גַּסּוּת הָרוּחַ, וַאֲפִלּוּ מִקְצָתָהּ.

וְכֵן הַכַּעַס, מִדָּה רָעָה הִיא עַד לִמְאֹד, וְרָאוּי לָאָדָם שֶׁיִּתְרַחֵק מִמֶּנָּה עַד
הַקָּצֶה הָאַחֵר. וִילַמֵּד עַצְמוֹ שֶׁלֹּא יִכְעַס, וַאֲפִלּוּ עַל דָּבָר שֶׁרָאוּי לִכְעֹס
עָלָיו. וְאִם רָצָה לְהַטִּיל אֵימָה עַל בָּנָיו וּבְנֵי בֵּיתוֹ, אוֹ עַל הַצִּבּוּר, אִם הָיָה
פַּרְנָס, וְרָצָה לִכְעֹס עֲלֵיהֶן כְּדֵי שֶׁיַּחְזְרוּ לַמּוּטָב – יַרְאֶה עַצְמוֹ בִּפְנֵיהֶם
שֶׁהוּא כּוֹעֵס כְּדֵי לְיַסְּרָם, וְתִהְיֶה דַּעְתּוֹ מְיֻשֶּׁבֶת בֵּינוֹ לְבֵין עַצְמוֹ, כְּאָדָם
שֶׁהוּא מְדַמֶּה כּוֹעֵס בִּשְׁעַת כַּעֲסוֹ, וְהוּא אֵינוֹ כּוֹעֵס. אָמְרוּ חֲכָמִים
הָרִאשׁוֹנִים: כָּל הַכּוֹעֵס כְּאִלּוּ עוֹבֵד עֲבוֹדָה זָרָה. וְאָמְרוּ: שֶׁכָּל הַכּוֹעֵס, אִם
חָכָם הוּא – חָכְמָתוֹ מִסְתַּלֶּקֶת מִמֶּנּוּ, וְאִם נָבִיא הוּא – נְבוּאָתוֹ מִסְתַּלֶּקֶת
מִמֶּנּוּ. וּבַעֲלֵי כַּעַס, אֵין חַיֵּיהֶם חַיִּים.

There are temperaments with regard to which a man is forbidden to follow the middle path. He should move away from one extreme and adopt the other.

Among these is arrogance. If a man is only humble, he is not following a good path. Rather, he must hold himself lowly and his spirit very unassuming. That is why Scripture describes our teacher Moses as "very humble" and not simply "humble." Therefore, our sages directed, "Hold oneself very, very lowly." Also, they declared, "Whoever is arrogant is as if he denied G-d's presence, as implied by the verse, 'And your heart will be haughty, and you will forget G-d, your L-rd.'" Furthermore, they said, "Whoever is arrogant should be placed under a ban of ostracism. This applies even if he is only somewhat arrogant."

Anger is also an exceptionally bad quality. It is appropriate that one move away from it and adopt the opposite extreme. He should school himself not to become angry even when it is fitting to be angry. If he should wish to arouse fear in his children and household—or within the community, if he is a communal leader—and wishes to be angry at them to motivate them to return to the proper path, he should present an angry front to them to punish them, but he should be inwardly calm. He should be like one who acts out the part of an angry man in his wrath, but is not himself angry.

The early sages said, "Anyone who becomes angry is like one who worships idols." They also said, "Whenever one becomes angry, if he is a wise man, his wisdom leaves him; if he is a prophet, his prophecy leaves him. The life of the irate is not true life."

3.

Bo

Tending to G-d's Children

Parenting Isn't Only about You

Dedicated in loving memory of Nachum Chaim ben Menachem Mendel Bolinsky,
נחום חיים בן מנחם מענדל, *marking his yahrtzeit on 28 Teves.*

May the merit of the Torah study worldwide accompany his soul in the world of everlasting life and be a source of blessings to his family with much health, happiness, nachas, and success.

PARSHA OVERVIEW

Bo

The last three of the Ten Plagues are visited on Egypt: a swarm of locusts devours all the crops and greenery; a thick, palpable darkness envelops the land; and all the firstborn of Egypt are killed at the stroke of midnight of the fifteenth day of the month of Nisan.

G-d commands the first mitzvah to be given to the people of Israel: to establish a calendar based on the monthly rebirth of the moon. The Israelites are also instructed to bring a "Passover offering" to G-d: a lamb or kid is to be slaughtered, and its blood sprinkled on the doorposts and lintels of every Israelite home so that G-d should pass over these homes when He comes to kill the Egyptian firstborn. The roasted meat of the offering is to be eaten that night together with matzah (unleavened bread) and bitter herbs.

The death of the firstborn finally breaks Pharaoh's resistance, and he literally drives the Children of Israel from his land. So hastily do they depart that there is no time for their dough to rise, and the only provisions they take along are unleavened. Before they go, they ask their Egyptian neighbors for gold, silver, and garments—fulfilling the promise made to Abraham that his descendants would leave Egypt with great wealth.

The Children of Israel are commanded to consecrate all firstborn and to observe the anniversary of the Exodus each year by removing all leaven from their possession for seven days, eating matzah, and telling the story of their redemption to their children. They are also commanded to wear *tefilin* on the arm and head as a reminder of the Exodus and their resultant commitment to G-d.

I. THE CHALLENGES OF PARENTING

A Top Priority

TEXT 1a

BEREISHIT (GENESIS) 18:19

> כִּי יְדַעְתִּיו לְמַעַן אֲשֶׁר יְצַוֶּה אֶת בָּנָיו וְאֶת בֵּיתוֹ אַחֲרָיו, וְשָׁמְרוּ דֶּרֶךְ ה'
> לַעֲשׂוֹת צְדָקָה וּמִשְׁפָּט, לְמַעַן הָבִיא ה' עַל אַבְרָהָם אֵת אֲשֶׁר דִּבֶּר עָלָיו:

I have known him because he instructs his children and his household after him that they should keep the way of G-d to perform righteousness and justice. Therefore, G-d will bring upon Abraham [the blessings] He spoke concerning him.

TEXT 1b

THE REBBE, RABBI MENACHEM MENDEL SCHNEERSON, HAYOM YOM, 8 TAMUZ

> מָצִינוּ דְּעִקַּר חִבָּתוֹ שֶׁל הַקָּדוֹשׁ בָּרוּךְ הוּא לְאַבְרָהָם אָבִינוּ עָלָיו הַשָּׁלוֹם
> הָיָה "לְמַעַן אֲשֶׁר יְצַוֶּה – כְּפֵרוּשׁוֹ, יְחַבֵּר – אֶת בָּנָיו וְאֶת בֵּיתוֹ". הַיְינוּ,
> דְּכָל גּוֹדֶל עֲבוֹדָתוֹ בְּהַנִּסְיוֹנוֹת אֵינוֹ בְּעֶרֶךְ לְגַבֵּי הָא דְיְצַוֶּה וִיחַבֵּר אֲחֵרִים,
> מַה שֶּׁיְזַכֶּה אֲחֵרִים.

G-d cherished Abraham primarily because "He instructs his children and his household." Now, the word "instructs" (*yetza-veh*) can also mean "connects." In other words, all of Abraham's achievements pale in comparison to his instructing and connecting others as well—making them, too, meritorious.

Hayom Yom

In 1942, Rabbi Yosef Yitzchak Schneersohn, the 6th rebbe of Chabad, gave his son-in-law, the future Rebbe, the task of compiling an anthology of Chasidic aphorisms and customs arranged according to the days of the year. In describing the completed product, Rabbi Yosef Yitzchak wrote that it is "a book that is small in format but bursting with pearls and diamonds of the choicest quality."

One Size Does Not Fit All

TEXT **2**

MALBIM, MISHLEI 22:6

> "חנך לנער על פי דרכו גם כי יזקין לא יסור ממנה": מצווה שיהיה
> החינוך על פי דרכו. כי כל אדם מסוגל מטבעו לענין אחר, בין בדעות
> – יש שמוחם חד, ויש ששכלם ישר בלתי מחודד, וצריך ללמדם
> כפי ההכנה שנמצא בו. ובין במעשים – יש שמוכן לאומנות מיוחד,
> ולמידה מיוחדת, ויקבל אותה בקל, וזה יוכר בהנער לפי התשוקה. ולפי
> מה שמשתדל בעצמו באיזה דבר מיוחד – צריך לחנכו לפי דרכו ולפי
> הרושמים שיש בו אל מה שהוא מוכן אליה, שאז, לא יסור ממנה גם
> כי יזקין. לא כן אם יחנכוהו אל מה שהוא זולת טבעו.

Rabbi Meir Leibush Wisser (Malbim)
1809–1879

Rabbi, Hebrew grammarian, and Bible commentator. Born in Ukraine, Rabbi Wisser served as rabbi in several prestigious communities across Europe. His fame reached as far as the Jewish community of New York, which offered him the position of first chief rabbi of the city, an offer he rejected. He is best known for his commentary to the entire Bible, which was unprecedented in its scope and thoroughness. He placed great emphasis on explaining the precise meaning of every word in the Bible.

"Train a child according to his way; even when he grows old, he will not turn away from it."

Malbim: This means that education must be tailored to the student because every person is naturally adaptive to something else. Intellectually, some are sharp while others are more straightforward, and each needs to be taught accordingly. Or in skill set, each has their own particular niche where they can catch on easily and excel. An educator can identify these by examining what the student is naturally attracted to and strives for.

Once identified, the educator must tailor their instruction according to each student's intellectual makeup and skill set.

If one follows this approach, then "even when he grows old, he will not turn away from it." However, if one educates a child without taking their unique natural inclinations into account, the instruction will fail the test of time.

Learn to Teach

TEXT 3

RABBI SHALOM DOVBER SCHNEERSOHN, TORAT SHALOM, P. 54

אָט אַזוי ווי הנחת תפילין בכל יום איז אַ מצוה דאורייתא אויף יעדער
אידן, אָהן אַ חילוק צי אַ גדול שבתורה צי אַ איש פּשוט – אָט אַזוי איז
אַ חוב גמור אויף יעדער אידן טראכטן יעדער טאָג אַ האַלבע שעה
וועגן דעם חינוך פֿון קינדער, און טאָן אַלץ וואָס בכוחו איז צו טאָן, און
יתר מכפי כוחו, פּועל זיין בײַ די קינדער, אַז זיי זאָהלען גיין אין דעם
דרך וואָס מי איז זיי מדריך.

Just as putting on *tefilin* every day is a Scriptural commandment incumbent on every Jew, regardless of whether he is a
great Torah scholar or a simple person, so, too, it is an absolute
obligation for every Jew to dedicate time every day to thinking
about his children's education. One must do everything in their
power—and indeed, more than what is in their power—to see
to it that our children follow the path in which they are being guided.

**Rabbi Shalom Dovber
Schneersohn
(Rashab)
1860–1920**

Chasidic rebbe. Rabbi Shalom
Dovber became the 5th leader of
the Chabad movement upon the
passing of his father, Rabbi Shmuel
Schneersohn. He established the
Lubavitch network of *yeshivot* called
Tomchei Temimim. He authored many
volumes of Chasidic discourses and is
renowned for his lucid and thorough
explanations of kabbalistic concepts.

II. IT'S YOUR OBLIGATION

The Obligations of Parenting

TEXT 4

MALBIM, MISHLEI 22:6

> שיחנכו את הנער, והוא שירגילנו מנעוריו אל השלימות, אם בדעות,
> אם במעשים ובמידות. כי ההרגל שיורגל בנעוריו, יעשו בו חקוי עצום
> ורושם שמור בנפש, לא יסור גם לעת זקנה. לא כן החינוך שיתחנך
> בגדלותו, אין החקוי קבוע בנפש, וימוש ממנו לעת זקנתו.

One must begin educating their child from a very young age, training them to be wholesome. This training should include intellectual pursuits, proper behavior, and desirable character traits. It needs to begin early because whatever the child will be accustomed to from a young age will develop into strong habits and leave a great impression upon him or her for the rest of their lives. If the training begins at a later age, however, the habits will not become deeply embedded and, with the passing years, will eventually fade.

TEXT 5

RABBI YESHAYAHU HALEVI HOROWITZ, SHALAH, GATE OF LETTERS, CH. 4

> צריך להרגילו ולחנכו במידות טובות וישרות – מעת שיוכל לדבר.

One must begin to train and educate their child to develop good and upstanding character traits—from the moment they begin to talk.

TEXT 6

RABBI SHNEUR ZALMAN OF LIADI, SHULCHAN
ARUCH HARAV, ORACH CHAYIM 343:2

> אביו, כיון שהוא מצווה מדברי סופרים לחנך את בנו או בתו אפילו
> במצוות עשה משהגיעו לחינוך – כל שכן שמחוייב מדברי סופרים
> לגעור בהם ולהפרישם מלעבור על לא תעשה, ואפילו על איסור של
> דברי סופרים.

A father is responsible to educate his sons and daughters to observe all the commandments. Consequently, if he finds his child violating a commandment, he must ensure they stop and make sure they know that this is improper behavior. The above applies even to rabbinic edicts.

**Rabbi Yeshayahu
Halevi Horowitz
(*Shalah*)
1565–1630**

Kabbalist and author. Rabbi Horowitz was born in Prague and served as rabbi in several prominent Jewish communities, including Frankfurt am Main and his native Prague. After the passing of his wife in 1620, he moved to Israel. In Tiberias, he completed his *Shenei Luchot Haberit*, an encyclopedic compilation of kabbalistic ideas. He is buried in Tiberias, next to Maimonides.

**Rabbi Shneur Zalman of Liadi
(Alter Rebbe)
1745–1812**

Chasidic rebbe, halachic authority, and founder of the Chabad movement. The Alter Rebbe was born in Liozna, Belarus, and was among the principal students of the Magid of Mezeritch. His numerous works include the *Tanya*, an early classic containing the fundamentals of Chabad Chasidism; and *Shulchan Aruch HaRav*, an expanded and reworked code of Jewish law.

Proxy Parenting—Redeeming the Firstborn

TEXT 7

TALMUD TRACTATE KIDUSHIN, 29A

> האב חייב בבנו למולו, ולפדותו, וללמדו תורה, ולהשיאו אשה, וללמדו
> אומנות. ויש אומרים: אף להשיטו במים.

A father is obligated to circumcise him, to redeem him, to teach him Torah, to marry him off, and to teach him a trade. And some say a father is also obligated to teach his son to swim.

Babylonian Talmud

A literary work of monumental proportions that draws upon the legal, spiritual, intellectual, ethical, and historical traditions of Judaism. The 37 tractates of the Babylonian Talmud contain the teachings of the Jewish sages from the period after the destruction of the 2nd Temple through the 5th century CE. It has served as the primary vehicle for the transmission of the Oral Law and the education of Jews over the centuries; it is the entry point for all subsequent legal, ethical, and theological Jewish scholarship.

TEXT 8a

SHEMOT (EXODUS) 13:1–2

> וַיְדַבֵּר ה' אֶל מֹשֶׁה לֵּאמֹר:
> קַדֶּשׁ לִי כָל בְּכוֹר פֶּטֶר כָּל רֶחֶם בִּבְנֵי יִשְׂרָאֵל, בָּאָדָם וּבַבְּהֵמָה, לִי הוּא:

G-d spoke to Moses, saying,

"Sanctify every firstborn to Me, every one that opens the womb [firstborn to their mother] among the Children of Israel, among man and among animals; they are all Mine."

TEXT 8b

IBID., 13:13

וְכָל פֶּטֶר חֲמֹר תִּפְדֶּה בְשֶׂה, וְאִם לֹא תִפְדֶּה – וַעֲרַפְתּוֹ, וְכֹל בְּכוֹר אָדָם בְּבָנֶיךָ תִּפְדֶּה:

And you shall redeem every firstborn donkey with a lamb, and if you do not redeem [it], you shall decapitate it, and every firstborn of man among your sons, you shall redeem.

TEXT 9

MAIMONIDES, MISHNEH TORAH, LAWS OF PRIESTLY GIFTS 11:1, 6

מִצְוַת עֲשֵׂה לִפְדּוֹת כָּל אִישׁ מִיִּשְׂרָאֵל בְּנוֹ שֶׁהוּא בְּכוֹר לְאִמּוֹ הַיִּשְׂרְאֵלִית, שֶׁנֶּאֱמַר (שמות לד יט): "כָּל פֶּטֶר רֶחֶם לִי". וְנֶאֱמַר (במדבר יח טו): "אַךְ פָּדֹה תִפְדֶּה אֵת בְּכוֹר הָאָדָם".

מִצְוָה זוֹ נוֹהֶגֶת בְּכָל מָקוֹם וּבְכָל זְמַן. וּבְכַמָּה פּוֹדֵהוּ? בְּחָמֵשׁ סְלָעִים, שֶׁנֶּאֱמַר (במדבר יח טז): "וּפְדוּיָו מִבֶּן חֹדֶשׁ תִּפְדֶּה".

Rabbi Moshe ben Maimon (Maimonides, Rambam) 1135–1204

Halachist, philosopher, author, and physician. Maimonides was born in Córdoba, Spain. After the conquest of Córdoba by the Almohads, he fled Spain and eventually settled in Cairo, Egypt. There, he became the leader of the Jewish community and served as court physician to the vizier of Egypt. He is most noted for authoring the *Mishneh Torah*, an encyclopedic arrangement of Jewish law; and for his philosophical work, *Guide for the Perplexed*. His rulings on Jewish law are integral to the formation of halachic consensus.

By a biblical positive command, each Israelite must redeem his son, the firstborn of an Israelite mother, as the verse states, "Every firstborn belongs to Me"; and it is written, "You shall have the firstborn of man redeemed."

This duty is applicable everywhere and at all times. For what price does he redeem him? For five shekels, as the verse states, "The redemption price for the child of one month is the equivalent of five shekels."

Who's Responsible?

Question for Discussion

Can we copy the above alternative reasonings for a father's obligation to his son and apply it to some of the other parental duties listed in Text 7? How would you apply it to the father's duty to circumcise his son, for example?

(Indeed, the same paradigm can be applied to both the obligation to circumcise and to teach one's son Torah.)

TEXT **10**

THE REBBE, RABBI MENACHEM MENDEL SCHNEERSON, LIKUTEI SICHOT 11, P. 45

> מהנפקא מינה לדינא בין שני האופנים: אם לא פדאו אביו בקטנותו עד
> שגדל הבן, על מי מהם מוטל חיוב הפדיה?
>
> דאם נימא כסברה הראשונה, שעיקר מצות הפדיון היא חובת הבן –
> הרי בנידון זה, שגדל הבן וכבר ראוי הוא – ולכן גם חייב הוא – לפדות
> את עצמו, נפקע חיובו (ובמילא גם זכותו) של האב בפדיית בנו בכורו.
> אבל אם נימא שהחיוב מעיקריה הוא על האב, הרי גם לאחר שגדל הבן
> ולא נפדה עדיין נשאר האב בחיובו ובזכותו.

Rabbi Menachem Mendel Schneerson
1902–1994

The towering Jewish leader of the 20th century, known as "the Lubavitcher Rebbe," or simply as "the Rebbe." Born in southern Ukraine, the Rebbe escaped Nazi-occupied Europe, arriving in the U.S. in June 1941. The Rebbe inspired and guided the revival of traditional Judaism after the European devastation, impacting virtually every Jewish community the world over. The Rebbe often emphasized that the performance of just one additional good deed could usher in the era of Mashiach. The Rebbe's scholarly talks and writings have been printed in more than 200 volumes.

One of the practical differences between the two approaches:

If the father, for whatever reason, neglected to redeem his first-born while a baby, who would be obligated to pay the five coins when the child grows into an adult?

According to the first approach—that the "redemption" is essentially the son's mitzvah—the adult son would naturally be *obligated* to redeem himself and pay the money.

According to the second approach, however—that redeeming his son is the father's own mitzvah—even after the child turns into an adult, the father retains his obligation to perform the redemption.

III. THE MISSION OF PARENTING

G-d's Child

TEXT 11a

SHEMOT (EXODUS) 4:22

וְאָמַרְתָּ אֶל פַּרְעֹה, כֹּה אָמַר ה', בְּנִי בְכֹרִי יִשְׂרָאֵל:

And you shall say to Pharaoh, "So said G-d, 'My firstborn son is Israel.'"

TEXT 11b

DEVARIM (DEUTERONOMY) 14:1

בָּנִים אַתֶּם לַה' אֱלֹקֵיכֶם, לֹא תִתְגֹּדְדוּ, וְלֹא תָשִׂימוּ קָרְחָה בֵּין עֵינֵיכֶם לָמֵת:

You are children of the L-rd, your G-d. You shall neither cut yourselves nor make any baldness between your eyes for the dead.

TEXT 12

RASHI, TALMUD TRACTATE KIDUSHIN, 30B

> שלשה שותפין הן באדם: הקדוש ברוך הוא, ואביו ואמו. בזמן שאדם
> מכבד את אביו ואת אמו, אמר הקדוש ברוך הוא: מעלה אני עליהם
> כאילו דרתי ביניהם וכבדוני.
>
> "שלשה שותפין הן": מפרש בברייתא במסכת נדה: איש מזריע לובן
> שבו, אשה מזרעת אודם שבו, והקדוש ברוך הוא נופח בו נשמה, מראה
> עין, ושמיעת אוזן ודיבור.

Rabbi Shlomo Yitzchaki (Rashi)
1040–1105

Most noted biblical and Talmudic commentator. Born in Troyes, France, Rashi studied in the famed *yeshivot* of Mainz and Worms. His commentaries on the Pentateuch and the Talmud, which focus on the straightforward meaning of the text, appear in virtually every edition of the Talmud and Bible.

The sages taught: There are three partners in a person's creation: The Holy One, Blessed be He; the father; and the mother. When a person honors their father and mother, the Holy One, Blessed be He, says, "I ascribe credit to them as if I dwelt between them and they honored Me as well."

Rashi: "There are three partners." Elsewhere, the Talmud explains: The man gives forth the white parts in the baby, the woman provides the red, and G-d provides the soul, by "breathing" it into the baby. This soul is what enables the body to see, hear, and speak.

Question for Discussion

Imagine you are entrusted with caring for the child of someone you greatly respect and admire (a great mentor, a dear relative, a world leader, etc.). Visualize them personally charging you with providing the child whatever he or she needs to develop into the best version of themselves. How would you approach this task?

Consider the following questions: What values should I instill in this child? What are safe and healthy behaviors that I should encourage and others that I should restrict? Who should I allow to be around this child? How should I interact with him or her?

TEXT 13

THE REBBE, RABBI MENACHEM MENDEL SCHNEERSON,
TORAT MENACHEM 5747:2, P. 650

בסגנון אחר קצת: כל ילד יהודי הרי הוא בן של הקדוש ברוך הוא
("אבינו שבשמים"), והאב והאם הגשמיים הם רק שלוחיו של הקדוש
ברוך הוא, שניתן להם הזכות להוליד את הילד ולגדלו ולחנכו.

Every Jewish child is *G-d's* child (we call G-d "our Father in Heaven"). The biological father and mother are merely G-d's messengers who were given the merit to give birth to, raise, and educate this special child.

Motherhood

TEXT 14

THE REBBE, RABBI MENACHEM MENDEL SCHNEERSON,
SEFER HASICHOT 5750:2, P. 455

ולא עוד אלא שיש יתרון בהחינוך (והתוכחה) דנשים לגבי אנשים –
כיון שמצד טבע הנשים נעשית פעולתן בחינוך בלשון רכה, ומתוך
רגש של קירוב, אהבה וחיבה (יותר מאשר אצל האנשים), ורואים
במוחש (ובפרט בדורות האחרונים), שדוקא בדרך של קירוב ואהבה
("חנוך לנער על פי דרכו") גדולה יותר הצלחת החינוך.

Moreover, women have a special advantage over men when it comes to education (and even to discipline). The feminine qualities in women allow them to impart their guidance with intimate closeness, softspokenness, love, and affection (much more than a man can offer). This is especially pertinent in recent times, when it is precisely the loving and warm approach to education ("Train a child according to *his* way") that bears the most fruit.

The Job Description

TEXT 15

THE REBBE, RABBI MENACHEM MENDEL SCHNEERSON,
TORAT MENACHEM 5743:3, P. 1482

בסגנון אחר: "שלשה שותפים באדם – אביו, ואמו, והקדוש ברוך הוא".
וחלוקת השותפות היא באופן שהענינים הרוחניים של הילד (חינוכו)
הם תחת אחריותם של אביו ואמו, כלומר, שהקדוש ברוך הוא הפקיד
בידם "פיקדון" יקר ביותר – "חלק אלקה ממעל ממש", מתוך תקווה
שימלאו את תפקידם לדאוג שנשמתו של הילד תאיר אצלו בגלוי, כך
שיהיה ניכר בו הענין ד"ואתם תהיו לי ממלכת כהנים וגוי קדוש"; ואילו
הענינים הגשמיים של הילד – לזונו ולפרנסו, לדאוג לבריאותו, וכיוצא
בזה – הם תחת אחריותו של הקדוש ברוך הוא. ולכן, כאשר ההורים
ממלאים את חלקם בשותפות זו באופן המתאים (על ידי החינוך בדרך
התורה ומצוותיה), הרי גם הקדוש ברוך הוא ממלא את חלקו בשותפות
באופן המתאים (פרנסה, בריאות, וכיוצא בזה).

"There are three partners in the forming of a person: The person's father, mother, and G-d."

The division of responsibilities in this partnership is as follows:

The biological parents are responsible for the spiritual welfare of the child (education, for example). Meaning to say, G-d entrusted them with an extremely precious "deposit"—"a G-dly soul from On High"—with the hope and expectation that the parents will complete their assignment and see to it that this child's soul be overtly expressed in everything he or she does. A job well done means that when looking at this child, one should be able to identify that this is a member of the nation that was told by G-d, "And you shall be to Me a kingdom of princes and a holy nation."

But when it comes to the physical needs of the child—that he be properly fed, clothed, and be healthy, etc.—that is G-d's share of the partnership.

And when the parents observe their side of the partnership (by educating their child to be an upstanding Jew), then G-d observes His side of the partnership by providing the parents with all their needs (whether it be finances, health, etc.).

4.

Beshalach

Healthy Boundaries

The Gravity of Overstepping into the Mundane

Dedicated in loving memory of Mr. Seymour Hirschfield,
שלמה בן צבי, marking his yahrtzeit on 14 Shevat.

May the merit of the Torah study worldwide accompany his soul in the world
of everlasting life and be a source of blessings to his family with much health,
happiness, nachas, and success.

PARSHA OVERVIEW

Beshalach

Soon after allowing the Children of Israel to depart from Egypt, Pharaoh chases after them to force their return, and the Israelites find themselves trapped between Pharaoh's armies and the sea. G-d tells Moses to raise his staff over the water; the sea splits to allow the Israelites to pass through and then closes over the pursuing Egyptians. Moses and the Children of Israel sing a song of praise and gratitude to G-d.

In the desert, the people suffer thirst and hunger. They repeatedly complain to Moses and Aaron. G-d miraculously sweetens the bitter waters of Marah, and later has Moses bring forth water from a rock by striking it with his staff. He causes manna to rain down from the heavens before dawn each morning, and quails to appear in the Israelite camp each evening.

The Children of Israel are instructed to gather a double portion of manna on Friday, as none will descend on Shabbat, the divinely decreed day of rest. Some disobey and go to gather manna on the seventh day, but find nothing. Aaron preserves a small quantity of manna in a jar, as a testimony for future generations.

In Rephidim, the people are attacked by the Amalekites, who are defeated by Moses's prayers and an army raised by Joshua.

I. A SPATIAL SABBATH LIMITATION

The Techum

TEXT 1

SHEMOT (EXODUS) 16:28–29

עַד אָנָה מֵאַנְתֶּם לִשְׁמֹר מִצְוֹתַי וְתוֹרֹתָי:

רְאוּ כִּי ה' נָתַן לָכֶם הַשַּׁבָּת, עַל כֵּן הוּא נֹתֵן לָכֶם בַּיּוֹם הַשִּׁשִּׁי לֶחֶם יוֹמָיִם.
שְׁבוּ אִישׁ תַּחְתָּיו, אַל יֵצֵא אִישׁ מִמְּקֹמוֹ בַּיּוֹם הַשְּׁבִיעִי:

How long will you refuse to observe my commandments and my teachings? See, G-d has given you the Sabbath. Therefore, on the sixth day, He gives you bread for two days. Let each man remain in his place; no man should leave his place on the seventh day.

TEXT 2a

MAIMONIDES, MISHNEH TORAH, LAWS OF SABBATH 27:1

"אַל יֵצֵא אִישׁ מִמְּקֹמוֹ בַּיּוֹם הַשְּׁבִיעִי". מָקוֹם זֶה – הוּא תְּחוּם הָעִיר.

"No man should leave his place on the seventh day." The term "place" refers to the *techum*—the range beyond the city's limits [into which we may not venture on the Sabbath].

Rabbi Moshe ben Maimon (Maimonides, Rambam) 1135–1204

Halachist, philosopher, author, and physician. Maimonides was born in Córdoba, Spain. After the conquest of Córdoba by the Almohads, he fled Spain and eventually settled in Cairo, Egypt. There, he became the leader of the Jewish community and served as court physician to the vizier of Egypt. He is most noted for authoring the *Mishneh Torah*, an encyclopedic arrangement of Jewish law; and for his philosophical work, *Guide for the Perplexed*. His rulings on Jewish law are integral to the formation of halachic consensus.

Two Thousand Amah

TEXT 2b

MAIMONIDES, IBID.

וְלֹא נָתְנָה תּוֹרָה שִׁעוּר לִתְחוּם זֶה, אֲבָל חֲכָמִים הֶעֱתִיקוּ שֶׁתְּחוּם זֶה הוּא חוּץ לִשְׁנֵים עָשָׂר מִיל, כְּנֶגֶד מַחֲנֵה יִשְׂרָאֵל. וְכָךְ אָמַר לָהֶם משֶׁה רַבֵּנוּ: לֹא תֵּצְאוּ חוּץ לַמַּחֲנֶה.

וּמִדִּבְרֵי סוֹפְרִים – שֶׁלֹּא יֵצֵא אָדָם חוּץ לָעִיר אֶלָּא עַד אַלְפַּיִם אַמָּה, אֲבָל חוּץ לְאַלְפַּיִם אַמָּה – אָסוּר, שֶׁאַלְפַּיִם אַמָּה הוּא מִגְרַשׁ הָעִיר.

The Torah did not explicitly state the extent of this range. The sages, however, transmitted a tradition that the range extends to twelve *mil* beyond the city, a measure that corresponds with the size of the Jewish camp in the desert. Thus, Moses our teacher instructed, "Do not go out beyond the camp."

Our sages [further reduced the range from twelve *mil* and] ruled that a person may only venture two thousand *amah* beyond the city. They chose this range because it is the size of the pasture-land that the Torah allocates to all cities [and thus the space is associated with the city].

TEXT 2c

MAIMONIDES, MISHNEH TORAH, LAWS OF SABBATH 27:2

נִמְצֵאתָ לָמֵד, שֶׁמֻּתָּר לְאָדָם בְּשַׁבָּת לְהַלֵּךְ אֶת כָּל הָעִיר כֻּלָּהּ, אֲפִלּוּ הָיְתָה
כְּנִינְוֵה, בֵּין שֶׁהָיְתָה מֻקֶּפֶת חוֹמָה, בֵּין שֶׁלֹּא הָיְתָה מֻקֶּפֶת חוֹמָה. וְכֵן מֻתָּר
לוֹ לְהַלֵּךְ חוּץ לָעִיר אַלְפַּיִם אַמָּה לְכָל רוּחַ מֵרְבָּעוֹת, כְּטַבְלָה מְרֻבַּעַת, כְּדֵי
שֶׁיִּהְיֶה נִשְׂכָּר אֶת הַזָּוִיּוֹת.

It follows that a person may walk freely throughout the city, even if it is as large as Nineveh, irrespective of whether it is surrounded by a wall. In addition, we may walk two thousand *amah* in any direction beyond the city's limits. When calculating the city's limits, a square is drawn around the entire city; thus, the areas between its farthest corners are included.

TEXT 3

MAIMONIDES, MISHNEH TORAH, LAWS OF SABBATH 27:4

מִי שֶׁשָּׁבַת בְּדִיר שֶׁבַּמִּדְבָּר, אוֹ בְּסַהַר, אוֹ בִּמְעָרָה וְכַיּוֹצֵא בָּהֶן מֵרְשׁוּת
הַיָּחִיד – מְהַלֵּךְ אֶת כֻּלָּהּ וְחוּצָה לָהּ אַלְפַּיִם אַמָּה לְכָל רוּחַ בְּרִבּוּעַ. וְכֵן
הַשּׁוֹבֵת בִּבְקְעָה . . . יֵשׁ לוֹ לְהַלֵּךְ מִמְּקוֹמוֹ אַלְפַּיִם אַמָּה לְכָל רוּחַ בְּרִבּוּעַ.
הָיָה מְהַלֵּךְ בִּבְקְעָה וְאֵינוֹ יוֹדֵעַ תְּחוּם שַׁבָּת – מְהַלֵּךְ אַלְפַּיִם פְּסִיעוֹת
בֵּינוֹנִיּוֹת, וְזֶה הוּא תְּחוּם שַׁבָּת.

One who spends the Sabbath in a barn in the desert, in a corral, in a cave, or in a similar type of private domain, may walk through its entire space and may continue to the limits of a square extending two thousand *amah* in every direction [from that domain]. Similarly, one who spends the Sabbath in an open valley . . . may walk to the limits of a square extending two thousand cubits in every direction from the place at which he is located at the commencement of the Sabbath. One who is walking in an open valley and does not know how far his Sabbath range extends may take two thousand ordinary steps. This is his Sabbath range.

Rabbinic Origin

TEXT 4

RASHI, SHEMOT (EXODUS) 16:29

"אל יצא איש ממקומו": אלו אלפים אמה של תחום שבת, ולא
במפורש, שאין תחומין אלא מדברי סופרים, ועיקרו של מקרא על
לוקטי המן נאמר.

"No man should leave his place." These are the two thousand
amah of the Sabbath range, but this is not explicit for the Sabbath range; rather, it is a rabbinic enactment. This verse was
primarily intended to reprimand the gatherers of manna.

**Rabbi Shlomo Yitzchaki
(Rashi)
1040–1105**

Most noted biblical and Talmudic
commentator. Born in Troyes, France,
Rashi studied in the famed *yeshivot* of
Mainz and Worms. His commentaries
on the Pentateuch and the Talmud,
which focus on the straightforward
meaning of the text, appear in virtually
every edition of the Talmud and Bible.

II. NOT BECOMING ADRIFT

Shevut *on the Sabbath*

TEXT **5**

MAIMONIDES, MISHNEH TORAH, LAWS OF SABBATH 21:1

נאמר בתורה "תשבות" – אפילו מדברים שאינם מלאכה חייב לשבות
מהם. ודברים הרבה הם שאסרו חכמים משום שבות. מהם – דברים
אסורים מפני שהם דומים למלאכות, ומהם – דברים אסורים, גזרה
שמא יבוא מהם מהם איסור סקילה.

The Torah tells us to cease during the Sabbath. This means that we must cease even from activities that are not included in the categories of forbidden labors. [The Torah left the definition of the scope of this commandment to] the sages, [who] forbade many activities under the rubric of *shevut*. Some activities are forbidden because they resemble the forbidden labors, while other activities are forbidden lest they lead one to commit a forbidden labor.

Learning Activity

Write down the two reasons for rabbinic restrictions on Shabbos.

_____

_____

_____

Not in the Spirit of the Day

TEXT **6**

MAIMONIDES, MISHNEH TORAH, LAWS OF SABBATH 24:1

יֵשׁ דְּבָרִים שֶׁהֵם אֲסוּרִין בְּשַׁבָּת, אַף עַל פִּי שֶׁאֵינָם דּוֹמִין לִמְלָאכָה וְאֵינָם
מְבִיאִין לִידֵי מְלָאכָה. וּמִפְּנֵי מָה נֶאֶסְרוּ? מִשׁוּם שֶׁנֶּאֱמַר: "אִם תָּשִׁיב
מִשַּׁבָּת רַגְלֶךָ עֲשׂוֹת חֲפָצֶיךָ בְּיוֹם קָדְשִׁי . . . וְכִבַּדְתּוֹ מֵעֲשׂוֹת דְּרָכֶיךָ,
מִמְּצוֹא חֶפְצְךָ וְדַבֵּר דָּבָר". לְפִיכָךְ, אָסוּר לְאָדָם לְהַלֵּךְ בַּחֲפָצָיו בְּשַׁבָּת,
וַאֲפִלּוּ לְדַבֵּר בָּהֶם, כְּגוֹן שֶׁיְדַבֵּר עִם שֻׁתָּפוֹ מַה יִּמְכֹּר לְמָחָר, אוֹ מַה יִּקְנֶה,
אוֹ הֵיאַךְ יִבְנֶה בַּיִת זֶה, וּבְאֵיזוֹ סְחוֹרָה יֵלֵךְ לְמָקוֹם פְּלוֹנִי – כָּל זֶה וְכַיּוֹצֵא
בּוֹ אָסוּר, שֶׁנֶּאֱמַר: "וְדַבֵּר דָּבָר".

There are activities that are forbidden on the Sabbath, though they don't resemble the forbidden labors nor do they lead to their performance. Why are these activities forbidden? Because it is written, "If you restrain your feet because of the Sabbath and refrain from pursuing your desires on My holy day . . . and you should honor it by refraining from following your ordinary ways, attending to your wants, and discussing mundane matters." Accordingly, it is forbidden to tend to our concerns on the Sabbath, or even to talk about them—to consult a partner on which merchandise should be sold the next day, or which should be purchased, how this building should be constructed, or which merchandise should be taken to a particular place. Such discussions are included in the prohibition against "discussing mundane matters."

TEXT 7

RABBI YECHIEL MICHEL HALEVI EPSTEIN, ARUCH
HASHULCHAN, ORACH CHAYIM 397:4

אבל תחומין – נראה דחכמים לא רצו שהאיש הישראלי ילך הרבה
בשבת כבחול, ויתעסק יותר בעונג שבת ובתורה.

With respect to the Sabbath boundaries, it appears that our
sages did not want Jews to stroll about excessively on the Sabbath as one does during the weekday. For it is proper to plug
into the delight of the Sabbath and engage in Torah study.

Rabbi Yechiel Michel Halevi Epstein
1829–1908

Noted author on Jewish law. Rabbi
Epstein lived in Czarist Lithuania and
was chief rabbi of Novozybkov, a town
near Minsk, and later, of Navahrudak,
where he served until his death. A
prolific writer, his primary work is
Aruch Hashulchan, an expanded and
reworked code of Jewish law.

III. THE *TECHUM* OF LIFE

Puncturing the Sabbath

TEXT 8

SEFER HACHINUCH, MITZVAH 32

> משרשי מצווה זו, שנהיה פנויים מעסקינו לכבוד היום, לקבוע
> בנפשותינו אמונת חידוש העולם, שהיא חבל המושכת כל יסודי
> הדת. ונזכור ביום אחד בכל שבוע ושבוע שהעולם נברא בששת ימים
> חלקים, ובשביעי לא נברא דבר . . . כשישבתו בני אדם כולם ביום אחד
> בשבוע, וישאל כל שואל: מה עילת זאת המנוחה? ויהיה המענה "כי
> ששת ימים עשה ה' וגו'", כל אחד יתחזק מתוך כך באמונה האמיתית.

Sefer Hachinuch

A work on the biblical commandments. Four aspects of every mitzvah are discussed in this work: the definition of the mitzvah; ethical lessons that can be deduced from the mitzvah; basic laws pertaining to the observance of the mitzvah; and who is obligated to perform the mitzvah, and when. The work was composed in the 13th century by an anonymous author who refers to himself as "the Levite of Barcelona." It has been widely thought that this referred to Rabbi Aharon Halevi of Barcelona (Re'ah); however, this view has been contested.

The root idea of this commandment is to withdraw from our engagements in honor of this day and affix within our souls the belief in the Creation of the world, which is the string that draws the foundations of our faith. That we should remember for one day each week that the world was created in six separate days and that on the seventh day, nothing was created. . . . When everyone rests for one day each week and someone asks why we rest, the answer—that we rest because G-d created the world in six days and rested on the seventh—reinforces the true faith among us all.

TEXT 9a

THE REBBE, RABBI MENACHEM MENDEL SCHNEERSON, LIKUTEI SICHOT 11, P. 70

> האיסור דמלאכת שבת, ענינו הוא, שבעשיית מלאכה מחלל הוא את
> השבת – עושה חלל ומקום פנוי בשבת, ובמילא מתחללת קדושתה;
> היינו שעל ידי המלאכה בשבת, מכניס בה ענין בלתי רצוי – "מכניס
> קליפה בשבת".

The idea behind the restriction against work on the Sabbath is that by performing creative activities, we form a space in the Sabbath that is devoid of holiness. That is to say, our activity introduces something inappropriate—something impure—into the Sabbath.

Rabbi Menachem Mendel Schneerson 1902–1994

The towering Jewish leader of the 20th century, known as "the Lubavitcher Rebbe," or simply as "the Rebbe." Born in southern Ukraine, the Rebbe escaped Nazi-occupied Europe, arriving in the U.S. in June 1941. The Rebbe inspired and guided the revival of traditional Judaism after the European devastation, impacting virtually every Jewish community the world over. The Rebbe often emphasized that the performance of just one additional good deed could usher in the era of Mashiach. The Rebbe's scholarly talks and writings have been printed in more than 200 volumes.

Exporting Shabbat Too Far Afield

TEXT **9b**

THE REBBE, RABBI MENACHEM MENDEL SCHNEERSON, IBID.

אִיסוּר דְּיצִיאָה חוּץ לַתְּחוּם – אֵין זֶה שֶׁהוּא מַכְנִיס עִנְיָן שֶׁל חוֹל בְּשַׁבָּת, אֶלָּא אַדְּרַבָּה, הוּא מוֹצִיא אֶת הַשַּׁבָּת לִמְקוֹם הַקְּלִיפּוֹת. כִּי בְּכָל אִישׁ מִבְּנֵי יִשְׂרָאֵל, גַּם בְּבוּר וְעַם הָאָרֶץ גָּמוּר, מֵאִיר אוֹר קְדוּשַׁת שַׁבָּת. וּכְשֶׁיּוֹצֵא חוּץ לַתְּחוּם (דִּקְדוּשָׁה), הֲרֵי הוּא מוֹצִיא עִמּוֹ גַּם אֶת קְדוּשַׁת הַשַּׁבָּת לִמְקוֹם הַקְּלִיפּוֹת.

The reason for the prohibition against walking beyond the Sabbath range is not that we introduce a weekday element into the Sabbath. Rather, it is that we export the Sabbath into the realm of unholiness. This is because within every Jew, even one who is boorish and completely ignorant, the radiance of the Sabbath is aglow. And when we step beyond the Sabbath boundaries, we bring the holiness of the Sabbath [that is within us] into the realm of unholiness.

Puncturing Your Personal Shabbat

TEXT 10a

THE REBBE, RABBI MENACHEM MENDEL SCHNEERSON, LIKUTEI SICHOT 11, P. 72

וכאשר האדם מכניס עובדין דחול לתוך מוחו ושכלו (בחינת שבת
שבו), הרי שנעשה בהם חלל ומקום פנוי . . . מהרגש אלוקי. דאילו
היה יודע ומרגיש את האמת אשר רק ברכת ה' היא תעשיר, ועשיית
העסק אינה אלא כלי לברכת ה' . . . לא היה מכניס את ראשו בהעסק,
בהמצאות ותחבולות שונות אשר ללא תועלת הן (מאחר שברכת ה'
היא תעשיר). ואדרבה, עסקיו אלו המרובים, המטרידים אותו מעניני
תורה ועבודה, הם המונעים ומעכבים מלהיות כלי ראוי לברכת ה'.

When we introduce worldly thinking into our minds (the Shabbos element within us), a void and emptiness is introduced that doesn't sense or feel G-dliness. For if we knew and felt the truth—that only G-d's blessing can make us wealthy and that our efforts are merely to form a vessel for His blessing—we would not invest our brains into business by scheming creative machinations and tactics that are, in any event, ineffective (for only G-d's blessing can grant success). On the contrary, becoming too engrossed in our many business affairs distracts us from Torah and serving G-d, which, in turn, prevents us from becoming proper vessels for the Divine's blessing.

Exporting Your Personal Shabbat Too Far Afield

TEXT 10b

THE REBBE, RABBI MENACHEM MENDEL SCHNEERSON, IBID.

והנה גם מי שאינו מכניס את עסקיו לתוך ה"שבת" שלו, עליו לדעת
שישנה עוד אזהרה: "איסור יציאה חוץ לתחום" – אשר "בשבת"
(בזמן השייך לתורה ומצוות) הרי גם בכוחות החיצונים שלו אסור
לצאת חוץ לתחום – אסור לצאת ברגליו (כוחותיו החיצונים) חוץ לענין
התורה ומצוות – כי התורה צריכה להיות ערוכה בכל רמ"ח איברים.

Even if we don't allow our business concerns to invade our
[inner] Sabbath, we must remember that there is yet another
restriction: the restriction against venturing beyond the bound-
ary. That is to say, during our Sabbath moments (times reserved
for Torah and *mitzvot*), even the outer aspect of our being, such
as our hands and feet, may not leave the boundaries to do
something unrelated to Torah and *mitzvot*. For the Torah must
permeate our entire body [not just the mind].

Elisha Ben Avuya's Techum Moment

TEXT 11

JERUSALEM TALMUD TRACTATE CHAGIGAH, 2:1

> רבי מאיר הוה יתיב דרש בבית מדרשא דטיבריה, עבר אלישע רביה
> רכיב על סוסייא ביום שובתא. אתון ואמרין ליה: הא רבך לבר. פסק ליה
> מן דרשה ונפק . . . אמר ליה: דייך מאיר, עד כאן תחום שבת. אמר ליה:
> מן הן את ידע? אמר ליה: מן טלפי דסוסיי דהוינא מני והולך אלפיים
> אמה. אמר ליה: וכל הדא חכמתא אית ביך, ולית את חזר בך?

Jerusalem Talmud

A commentary to the Mishnah, compiled during the 4th and 5th centuries. The Jerusalem Talmud predates its Babylonian counterpart by 100 years and is written in both Hebrew and Aramaic. While the Babylonian Talmud is the most authoritative source for Jewish law, the Jerusalem Talmud remains an invaluable source for the spiritual, intellectual, ethical, historical, and legal traditions of Judaism.

One Sabbath, Rabbi Meyer was sitting in a house of study in Tiberius and teaching when his teacher Elisha passed the study house on horseback. They came and told Rabbi Meyer, "Your teacher is outside." Rabbi Meyer stopped the lecture and stepped out. [They walked together for a while and conversed.] . . .

Elisha said to him, "Meyer, this is as far as you can go; we have reached the outer limits of the Sabbath range."

Rabbi Meyer replied, "How do you know?"

Elisha replied, "I have been counting my horse's steps and know that we have traveled two thousand *amah*."

Rabbi Meyer said, "You have so much wisdom; would you not turn back?"

5.

Yisro

Lift Your Hands above Your Head

Reaching the Pinnacle of Human Achievement . . . and Beyond

Dedicated in loving memory of Reb Moshe Yosef Nechemia Eisenstadt,
ר' משה יוסף נחמיה בן ר' מנחם צבי ז"ל, *marking his* yahrtzeit *on 18 Shevat.*

May the merit of the Torah study worldwide accompany his soul in the world of everlasting life and be a source of blessings to his family with much health, happiness, nachas, and success.

PARSHA OVERVIEW

Yisro

Moses's father-in-law, Jethro, hears of the great miracles that G-d performed for the people of Israel and comes from Midian to the Israelite camp, bringing with him Moses's wife and two sons. Jethro advises Moses to appoint a hierarchy of magistrates and judges to assist him in the task of governing and administering justice to the people.

The Children of Israel camp opposite Mount Sinai, where they are told that G-d has chosen them to be His "kingdom of priests" and "holy nation." The people respond by proclaiming, "All that G-d has spoken, we shall do."

On the sixth day of the third month (Sivan), seven weeks after the Exodus, the entire nation of Israel assembles at the foot of Mount Sinai. G-d descends on the mountain amidst thunder, lightning, billows of smoke, and the blast of the *shofar* and summons Moses to ascend.

G-d proclaims the Ten Commandments, commanding the people of Israel to believe in G-d, not to worship idols or take G-d's name in vain, to keep the Shabbat, to honor their parents, not to murder, not to commit adultery, not to steal, and not to bear false witness or covet another's property. The people cry out to Moses that the revelation is too intense for them to bear, begging him to receive the Torah from G-d and convey it to them.

I. COULDN'T DO IT WITHOUT HIM

Introduction

TEXT 1

SHEMOT (EXODUS) 18:1, 5, 8–12

וַיִּשְׁמַע יִתְרוֹ כֹהֵן מִדְיָן חֹתֵן מֹשֶׁה, אֵת כָּל אֲשֶׁר עָשָׂה אֱלֹקִים לְמֹשֶׁה
וּלְיִשְׂרָאֵל עַמּוֹ, כִּי הוֹצִיא ה' אֶת יִשְׂרָאֵל מִמִּצְרָיִם: . . .

וַיָּבֹא יִתְרוֹ חֹתֵן מֹשֶׁה וּבָנָיו וְאִשְׁתּוֹ אֶל מֹשֶׁה, אֶל הַמִּדְבָּר אֲשֶׁר הוּא חֹנֶה
שָׁם הַר הָאֱלֹקִים: . . .

וַיְסַפֵּר מֹשֶׁה לְחֹתְנוֹ אֵת כָּל אֲשֶׁר עָשָׂה ה' לְפַרְעֹה וּלְמִצְרַיִם עַל אוֹדֹת
יִשְׂרָאֵל, אֵת כָּל הַתְּלָאָה אֲשֶׁר מְצָאָתַם בַּדֶּרֶךְ, וַיַּצִּלֵם ה':

וַיִּחַדְּ יִתְרוֹ עַל כָּל הַטּוֹבָה אֲשֶׁר עָשָׂה ה' לְיִשְׂרָאֵל, אֲשֶׁר הִצִּילוֹ מִיַּד מִצְרָיִם:

וַיֹּאמֶר יִתְרוֹ, בָּרוּךְ ה' אֲשֶׁר הִצִּיל אֶתְכֶם מִיַּד מִצְרַיִם וּמִיַּד פַּרְעֹה, אֲשֶׁר
הִצִּיל אֶת הָעָם מִתַּחַת יַד מִצְרָיִם:

עַתָּה יָדַעְתִּי כִּי גָדוֹל ה' מִכָּל הָאֱלֹהִים, כִּי בַדָּבָר אֲשֶׁר זָדוּ עֲלֵיהֶם:

וַיִּקַּח יִתְרוֹ חֹתֵן מֹשֶׁה עֹלָה וּזְבָחִים לֵאלֹקִים, וַיָּבֹא אַהֲרֹן וְכֹל זִקְנֵי יִשְׂרָאֵל,
לֶאֱכָל לֶחֶם עִם חֹתֵן מֹשֶׁה, לִפְנֵי הָאֱלֹקִים:

Now Moses's father-in-law, Jethro, the chieftain of Kohen, heard all that G-d had done for Moses and for Israel, His people, and that G-d had taken Israel out of Egypt. . . .

Now Moses's father-in-law, Jethro, and his [Moses's] sons and his wife came to Moses, to the desert where he was encamped, to the mountain of G-d. . . .

Moses told his father-in-law [about] all that G-d had done to Pharaoh and to the Egyptians on account of Israel, [about] all the hardships that had befallen them on the way, and [that] G-d had saved them.

Jethro was happy about all the good that G-d had done for Israel, that He had rescued them from the hands of the Egyptians.

[Thereupon,] Jethro said, "Blessed is G-d, Who has rescued you from the hands of the Egyptians and from the hand of Pharaoh and Who has rescued the people from beneath the hand of the Egyptians.

"Now I know that G-d is greater than all the deities, for with the thing that they plotted, [He came] upon them."

Then Moses's father-in-law, Jethro, sacrificed burnt offering[s] and [peace] offerings to G-d, and Aaron and all the elders of Israel came to dine with Moses's father-in-law before G-d.

TEXT **2**

MECHILTA, AD LOC.

> "כֹּהֵן מִדְיָן": רַבִּי יְהוֹשֻׁעַ אוֹמֵר: כֹּמֶר הָיָה . . . רַבִּי אֶלְעָזָר הַמּוֹדָעִי אוֹמֵר: שַׂר הָיָה.

"*Kohen* of Midian." Rabbi Yehoshua says, "He was a priest." . . . Rabbi Elazar says, "He was a minister."

Mechilta

A halachic Midrash to Exodus. Midrash is the designation of a particular genre of rabbinic literature usually forming a running commentary on specific books of the Bible. The name *Mechilta* means "rule" and was given to this Midrash because its comments and explanations are based on fixed rules of exegesis. This work is often attributed to Rabbi Yishmael ben Elisha, a contemporary of Rabbi Akiva, though there are some references to later sages in this work.

TEXT 3

RASHI, SHEMOT (EXODUS), 18:1

> "יתרו": שבע שמות נקראו לו: רעואל, יתר, יתרו, חובב, חבר, קיני,
> פוטיאל. **יתר** – על שם שיתר פרשה אחת בתורה, "ואתה תחזה". **יתרו**
> – לכשנתגייר וקיים המצות, הוסיפו לו אות אחת על שמו. **חובב** –
> שחיבב את התורה, וחובב הוא יתרו, שנאמר: "מבני חובב חותן משה".

Rabbi Shlomo Yitzchaki (Rashi)
1040–1105

Most noted biblical and Talmudic commentator. Born in Troyes, France, Rashi studied in the famed *yeshivot* of Mainz and Worms. His commentaries on the Pentateuch and the Talmud, which focus on the straightforward meaning of the text, appear in virtually every edition of the Talmud and Bible.

"Jethro." He was called by seven names: Reuel, Jether, Jethro [i.e., Yisro], Hobab, Heber, Keni, [and] Putiel. [He was called] Jether (יֶתֶר) because he [caused] a section to be added (יִתֵּר) to the Torah, [namely,] "But you shall choose." [He was called] Jethro (יִתְרוֹ) [to indicate that] when he converted and fulfilled the commandments, a letter was added to his name. [He was called] Hobab (חוֹבָב), [which means lover,] because he loved (חָבַב) the Torah. Hobab was indeed Jethro, as it is said, "Of the children of Hobab, Moses's father-in-law."

Question—Precursor to the Torah?

TEXT 4

ZOHAR 2:67B–68A

> אתא יתרו כומרא עילאה ורברבא, רב ממנא (דכל ממנא) דכל טעוון
> אחרנין, ואודי ליה לקודשא בריך הוא, ואמר: "עתה ידעתי כי גדול ה'
> מכל האלהים". כדין אסתלק ואתייקר קודשא בריך הוא ביקריה עילא
> ותתא, ולבתר יהב אורייתא בשלימו דשלטנו על כולא.

Zohar

The seminal work of kabbalah, Jewish mysticism. The *Zohar* is a mystical commentary on the Torah, written in Aramaic and Hebrew. According to the Arizal, the *Zohar* contains the teachings of Rabbi Shimon bar Yocha'i, who lived in the Land of Israel during the 2nd century. The *Zohar* has become one of the indispensable texts of traditional Judaism, alongside and nearly equal in stature to the Mishnah and Talmud.

Jethro, the greatest of all pagan priests, arrived and swore fealty to G-d, stating, "Now I know that G-d is greater than all the deities." At that moment, G-d's glory was resplendent in both the greatest heights and lowest realms. Thereafter, G-d gave a perfect Torah that reigns supreme over all else.

II. HANDS UP!

Personal Space in Halachah

TEXT 5

SHITAH LEMO'ED KATAN, P. 161

מקומו של אדם הוא ארבע אמות.

Four *amot* (cubits) surrounding a person are considered his or her personal space.

Acquires Belongings

TEXT 6

MAIMONIDES, MISHNEH TORAH, LAWS OF ROBBERY AND LOST OBJECTS 17:8–9

חצרו של אדם קונה לו שלא מדעתו, ואם נפלה בה מציאה – הרי היא
של בעל החצר . . .

ארבע אמות של אדם שהוא עומד בצידו – הרי אלו קונים לו, ואם
הגיעה המציאה לתוך ארבע אמות שלו – זכה בה.

חכמים תקנו דבר זה, כדי שלא יריבו המוצאין זה עם זה. במה דברים
אמורים? בסימטא, או בצידי רשות הרבים שאין הרבים דוחקין בהן, או
בשדה שאין לו בעלים. אבל העומד ברשות הרבים או בתוך שדה חבירו
– אין ארבע אמות קונות לו, ואינו קונה שם עד שתגיע מציאה לידו.

Rabbi Moshe ben Maimon (Maimonides, Rambam)
1135–1204

Halachist, philosopher, author, and physician. Maimonides was born in Córdoba, Spain. After the conquest of Córdoba by the Almohads, he fled Spain and eventually settled in Cairo, Egypt. There, he became the leader of the Jewish community and served as court physician to the vizier of Egypt. He is most noted for authoring the *Mishneh Torah,* an encyclopedic arrangement of Jewish law; and for his philosophical work, *Guide for the Perplexed.* His rulings on Jewish law are integral to the formation of halachic consensus.

A person's courtyard can acquire property for him without his being aware of it. Thus, if a lost object falls into a person's courtyard, he acquires it. . . .

Similarly, the area within a radius of four cubits next to the place where a person is standing can acquire property for him like his own courtyard. If a lost object comes into these four cubits, he acquires it.

Our sages ordained this convention so that people who discover lost articles should not come to strife.

When is this convention employed? In an alleyway or at the sides of the public domain, which are not crowded with many people, or in a field that is ownerless. When, however, a person stands in the public domain or in a field belonging to a colleague, the area within a radius of four cubits cannot acquire property on his behalf. In such a place, he cannot acquire a lost article until it reaches his hand.

TEXT 7

RABBI NISSIM OF GERONA, CHIDDUSHEI HARAN, TRACTATE GITIN, 87A

> ואף על גב דארבע אמות לכולי עלמא אינן קונות דבר תורה, כיון דרבנן
> תקנינהו ואמרו שיהו קונות – הרי הקנום לו ועשאום כחצירו, והפקר
> בית דין הפקר.

That the four *amot* surrounding a person function as a *kinyan* does not have Scriptural roots. Nevertheless, inasmuch as the rabbis enacted that these four *amot* acquire objects, using the power of the courts to seize property, the rabbis transfer ownership of the actual space to the person standing beside it like a *chatzer*.

Rabbi Nissim Gerondi (Ran)
1320–1376

Talmudist, halachic authority, and philosopher. Rabbi Nissim was born in Barcelona and lived in Gerona. He was one of the last of the great Spanish medieval Talmudic scholars. He did not hold any rabbinic post but served as a physician in the royal palace. His works include commentaries on Rabbi Yitzchak Alfasi's code, responsa literature, and a collection of sermons that elucidate fundamentals of Judaism.

Gitin and Kidushin

TEXT 8

MAIMONIDES, MISHNEH TORAH, LAWS OF DIVORCE 5:12

> הָיְתָה יָדָהּ קַטַפְרֵס וְזָרַק הַגֵּט עַל יָדָהּ וְנָפַל לָאָרֶץ, אִם נָפַל לְתוֹךְ אַרְבַּע
> אַמּוֹת שֶׁלָּהּ וְנָח – הֲרֵי זוֹ מְגֹרֶשֶׁת.

[The following rules apply if a woman holds] her hand at an incline, [her husband] throws a get to her hand, and it falls to the earth: if it falls within four *amot* of where she is standing and comes to rest there, the divorce is effective.

Shabbat Law

TEXT 9

MISHNAH TRACTATE EIRUVIN, 45A

> מי שישן בדרך ולא ידע שחשיכה . . . אין לו אלא ארבע אמות. רבי
> אלעזר אומר: והוא באמצען.

One who fell asleep while traveling and didn't realize that Shabbat arrived . . . is not allowed to travel further than four *amot*. Rabbi Elazar said, "He is the center of those four *amot*."

Mishnah

The first authoritative work of Jewish law that was codified in writing. The Mishnah contains the oral traditions that were passed down from teacher to student; it supplements, clarifies, and systematizes the commandments of the Torah. Due to the continual persecution of the Jewish people, it became increasingly difficult to guarantee that these traditions would not be forgotten. Rabbi Yehudah Hanassi therefore redacted the Mishnah at the end of the 2nd century. It serves as the foundation for the Talmud.

Prayer

TEXT 10

RABBI YOSEF CARO, SHULCHAN ARUCH, ORACH CHAYIM 102:1, 4

> אסור לישב בתוך ד' אמות של מתפלל, בין מלפניו בין מן הצדדין (ובין
> מלאחריו) צריך להרחיק ד' אמות . . .
> אסור לעבור כנגד המתפללים בתוך ד' אמות. ודווקא לפניהם, אבל
> בצידיהם – מותר לעבור ולעמוד.

One must not sit within the four *amot* of a person immersed in prayer. Whether in front, in back, or to the sides, one must distance themselves four *amot*. . . .

[Likewise,] one must not pass within the four *amot* in front of a person immersed in prayer. This restriction is limited to the front of the praying person alone.

Rabbi Yosef Caro (Maran, *Beit Yosef*) 1488–1575

Halachic authority and author. Rabbi Caro was born in Spain but was forced to flee during the Expulsion in 1492 and eventually settled in Safed, Israel. He authored many works, including the *Beit Yosef, Kesef Mishneh,* and a mystical work, *Magid Meisharim*. Rabbi Caro's magnum opus, the Shulchan Aruch (Code of Jewish Law), has been universally accepted as the basis for modern Jewish law.

Hands above Your Head

TEXT 11

TALMUD TRACTATE EIRUVIN, 48A

הני ד' אמות היכא כתיבא? כדתניא: "שבו איש תחתיו" – כתחתיו,
[וכמה תחתיו?] גופו שלש אמות, ואמה כדי לפשוט ידיו ורגליו, דברי
רב מאיר. רב יהודה אומר: גופו שלש אמות, ואמה כדי שיטול חפץ
מתחת מרגלותיו ומניח תחת מראשותיו.

Babylonian Talmud

A literary work of monumental proportions that draws upon the legal, spiritual, intellectual, ethical, and historical traditions of Judaism. The 37 tractates of the Babylonian Talmud contain the teachings of the Jewish sages from the period after the destruction of the 2nd Temple through the 5th century CE. It has served as the primary vehicle for the transmission of the Oral Law and the education of Jews over the centuries; it is the entry point for all subsequent legal, ethical, and theological Jewish scholarship.

What is the Scriptural source for the four *amot* within which a person is always permitted to walk on Shabbat?

As it was taught, [the verse states,] "Remain every man in his place; let no man go out of his place on the seventh day," [meaning one must restrict movement to an area] equal to his place. And how much is the area of his place? A body typically measures three *amot*, and an additional *amah* is needed to allow him to spread out his hands and feet; this is the statement of Rabbi Meir. Rabbi Yehudah says, "A person's body measures three *amot*, and an additional *amah* is needed in order to allow him to pick up an object from under his feet and place it by his head."

TEXT 12

THE REBBE, RABBI MENACHEM MENDEL SCHNEERSON, LIKUTEI SICHOT 16, P. 196

דער מענטש (ראשו, גופו ורגליו) מצד זיין בריאה פארנעמט ג' אמות
(וואס די ג' אמות זיינען כנגד ומרמז אויף די כלליות'דיקע ג' מדריגות
פון ראש, גוף, רגל); און מצד הבריאה איז דער ראש – כשמו – די
העכסטע מדריגה און מקום ביים מענטשן, נידעריקער דערפון איז
דער גוף, און די נידעריקסטע דרגא און מקום זיינען די רגליים.
דאס הייסט – מצד הבריאה זיינען די ידים, בײַ בײדע זײַטן פון גוף,
נידעריקער פון ראש.

די עבודה פון דעם אדם באשטייט אין דעם, ער זאל זיך אויפהויבן
העכער ווי (די ג' אמות וואס) מצד הבריאה, העכער וו די העכסטע
מדריגה אין זיין בריאה, וואס דאס איז דער ראש, דער מקום השכל;
דאס הייסט ער זאל מיט זיין הבנה והשגה (ניט בליֹיבן ביים גדר והגבלה
פון זיין "ראש" ושכל, נאר) זיין אריינגעטאן אין ענינים וואס זיינען
העכער פון זיין "ראש" מצד עצמו.

Rabbi Menachem Mendel Schneerson
1902–1994

The towering Jewish leader of the 20th century, known as "the Lubavitcher Rebbe," or simply as "the Rebbe." Born in southern Ukraine, the Rebbe escaped Nazi-occupied Europe, arriving in the U.S. in June 1941. The Rebbe inspired and guided the revival of traditional Judaism after the European devastation, impacting virtually every Jewish community the world over. The Rebbe often emphasized that the performance of just one additional good deed could usher in the era of Mashiach. The Rebbe's scholarly talks and writings have been printed in more than 200 volumes.

Naturally, a person takes up the space of three *amot*, corresponding to the three umbrella parts of the body, namely, the head, torso, and legs. According to the rules of Creation, the head is the loftiest part of the person, then the torso, and finally the lowest part—the legs. In this scheme, the hands, which extend out of both sides of the torso, are lower than the head.

It is each person's task to reach beyond the three *amot* designated to humanity at Creation, to reach beyond the peak of what a human can naturally achieve, namely, beyond the head, the seat of reason. In other words, a person should use his or her reason, and instead of getting stuck in the parameters of that very power of reason, break free and engage in matters that are beyond what the "head" can reach on its own.

III. BREAKING THE FOURTH WALL

Torah in Four Parts

TEXT 13

ZOHAR 3:152A

תא חזי: אית לבושא דאתחזי לכולא, ואינון טפשין כד חמאן לבר נש
בלבושא דאתחזי לון שפירא – לא מסתכלין יתיה. חשיבו דההוא
לבושא גופא. חשיבותא דגופא נשמתא. כהai גוונא אורייתא אית לה
גופא, ואינון פקודי אורייתא, דאקרון גופי תורה. האי גופא מתלבשא
בלבושין דאינון ספורין דהai עלמא. טפשין דעלמא לא מסתכלי אלא
בההוא לבושא דאיהו ספור דאורייתא, ולא ידעי יתיה, ולא מסתכלי
במה דאיהו תחות ההוא לבושא. אינון דידעין יתיר – לא מסתכלן
בלבושא, אלא בגופא דאיהו תחות ההוא לבושא. חכימין עבדי דמלכא
עילאה אינון דקיימו בטורא דסיני, לא מסתכלי אלא בנשמתא דאיהי
עיקרא דכולא אורייתא ממש.

Come, look: what a person wears is visible to all, and only the foolish will look at a person with nice clothing and look no further.

The body and its clothing are a metaphor for the body and soul.

The Torah has a body, namely, the *mitzvot*, which are very "dressed up" in the terms of our world, like a body in clothing. The foolish only look at the clothing, namely, the stories of the Torah, and do not bother looking to see what lies behind the clothing.

But those who know better do not suffice with looking at the clothing alone, rather at the body that lies underneath the clothing. The wise servants of the eternal King who stood at [Mount] Sinai looked only at the *soul* of Torah, the main part of Torah.

Reaching the Fourth Dimension of Torah

TEXT 14

MIDRASH TANCHUMA, VA'ERA 16

משל למה הדבר דומה? למלך שגזר ואמר: בני רומי לא ירדו לסוריא,
ובני סוריא לא יעלו לרומי. כן, כשברא הקדוש ברוך הוא את העולם, גזר
ואמר: "השמים שמים לה', והארץ נתן לבני אדם". שביקש ליתן את
התורה, ביטל את הגזרה הראשונה, ואמר: התחתונים יעלו לעליונים,
והעליונים ירדו לתחתונים.

To what is the matter analogous?

To a king who decreed, "The people of Rome cannot descend to
Syria, and the Syrians cannot ascend to Rome."

So, too, when G-d created the world, He decreed, "The Heavens
belong to G-d, and earth was given to humans." When G-d gave
the Torah, He abolished the decree, stating, "Those below shall
climb above, and those above shall descend below."

Jethro's Radicalism

TEXT 15

RASHI, SHEMOT (EXODUS) 18:1

"וישמע יתרו": מה שמועה שמע ובא? קריעת ים סוף ומלחמת עמלק.

"Jethro . . . heard." What news did he hear that [made such an
impression that] he came? The splitting of the Red Sea and the
war with Amalek.

Tanchuma

A Midrashic work bearing the name of
Rabbi Tanchuma, a 4th-century Talmudic
sage quoted often in this work. "Midrash"
is the designation of a particular genre
of rabbinic literature usually forming a
running commentary on specific books
of the Bible. *Tanchuma* provides textual
exegeses, expounds upon the biblical
narrative, and develops and illustrates
moral principles. *Tanchuma* is unique in
that many of its sections commence with
a halachic discussion, which subsequently
leads into nonhalachic teachings.

TEXT 16

THE REBBE, RABBI MENACHEM MENDEL SCHNEERSON,
LIKUTEI SICHOT 16, PP. 201–202

היות אז דער ענין פון מתן תורה איז . . . דער ביטול הגזירה, ביז אז
"תחתונים יעלו לעליונים" – נבראים זאלן ארויסגיין פון זייער גדר
אלס נבראים און אויפהייבן זיך העכער, לעליונים – איז דערפון
פארשטאנדיק, אז אויך ביי יתרו (וואס ביאתו איז געווען א הכנה צו
מתן תורה) איז געווען אט די עבודה מיט זיך אליין: ארויסגיין פון זיינע
מדידות והגבלות . . .

וואס האט אים אבער געבראכט ער זאל קומען: ער זאל ארויסגיין פון
זיינע הגבלות ביז צום קומען אין א מדבר שמם, א מקום תהו? . . .

די שמועה פון אט די צוויי ענינים – קריעת ים סוף ומלחמת עמלק
– האט באווירקט יתרו'ן ער זאל קומען – "ובא" – ער זאל ארויס פון
זיינע הגבלות, אוועקגיין פון זיין כבוד אלס "כהן מדין", און קומען
אין מדבר שמם כו' להתגייר; און אט דאס איז געווען די הכנה צו מתן
תורה, וועין ביטול הגזירה כו' און – תחתונים יעלו לעליונים.

The entire thrust of *Matan Torah* was about shatter-ing the Great Divide between the upper and lower worlds, namely, that a physical creature should be able to climb out of his or her natural limits and reach beyond into the Divine. As such, Jethro's personal odyssey (which, as mentioned, laid the groundwork for *Matan Torah*) mirrored this notion: he broke free of his personal limitations. . . .

[After all,] what made Jethro actually *come*? What compelled Jethro to shatter his personal limitations and join the Jews in a desolate desert? . . .

It was *this* idea, . . . namely, that Jethro was impacted in a way that he knew he had to actually *come*, to break free of his natural limitations, to give up his prestige as a Kohen of Midian, come to a desolate place, and convert.

This laid the groundwork for *Matan Torah*, when G-d shattered the Great Divide between the upper and lower worlds.

6.

Mishpatim

I Went in with an Escape Plan. It Didn't Work.

The Case for Going All-In

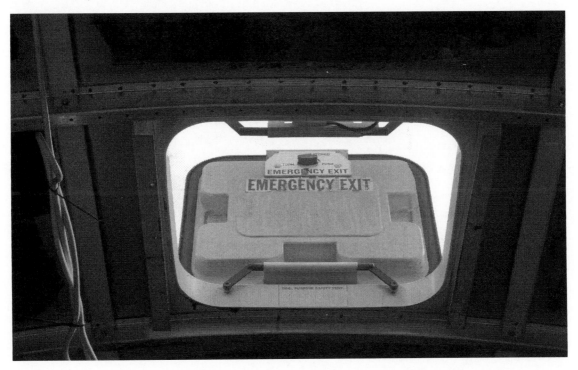

Dedicated to our dear friend and partner, Rabbi Mendel Kotlarsky on the occasion of his birthday on 28 Shevat.

May he go from strength to strength and enjoy good health, happiness, nachas from his loved ones, and success in all of his endeavors.

PARSHA OVERVIEW

Mishpatim

Following the revelation at Mount Sinai, G-d legislates a series of laws for the people of Israel. These include the laws of the indentured servant; the penalties for murder, kidnapping, assault, and theft; civil laws pertaining to redress of damages, the granting of loans, and the responsibilities of the "Four Guardians"; and the rules governing the conduct of courts of law in administering justice.

Also included are laws warning against mistreatment of foreigners, the observance of the seasonal festivals and the agricultural gifts that are to be brought to the Holy Temple in Jerusalem; the prohibition against cooking meat with milk, and the mitzvah of prayer. Altogether, the *parsha* of *Mishpatim* contains fifty-three *mitzvot*: twenty-three imperative commandments and thirty prohibitions.

G-d promises to bring the people of Israel to the Holy Land and warns them against assuming the pagan ways of its current inhabitants.

The people of Israel proclaim, "We will do and we will hear all that G-d commands us." Leaving Aaron and Hur in charge in the Israelite camp, Moses ascends Mount Sinai and remains there for forty days and forty nights to receive the Torah from G-d.

I. SLAVERY AS THE FIRST MITZVAH?

A Jewish Slave

TEXT 1

SHEMOT (EXODUS) 21:2, 5–6

כִּי תִקְנֶה עֶבֶד עִבְרִי, שֵׁשׁ שָׁנִים יַעֲבֹד, וּבַשְּׁבִיעִית יֵצֵא לַחָפְשִׁי חִנָּם: . . .

וְאִם אָמֹר יֹאמַר הָעֶבֶד, אָהַבְתִּי אֶת אֲדֹנִי, אֶת אִשְׁתִּי וְאֶת בָּנָי, לֹא אֵצֵא חָפְשִׁי:

וְהִגִּישׁוֹ אֲדֹנָיו אֶל הָאֱלֹהִים, וְהִגִּישׁוֹ אֶל הַדֶּלֶת אוֹ אֶל הַמְּזוּזָה, וְרָצַע אֲדֹנָיו אֶת אָזְנוֹ בַּמַּרְצֵעַ, וַעֲבָדוֹ לְעֹלָם:

Should you buy a Hebrew slave, he must work [for] six years, and in the seventh [year], he will be liberated without charge. . . . But if the slave says, "I love my master, my wife, and my children. I will not go free," his master will bring him before the judges and bring him to the door or to the doorpost, and his master will bore his ear with an awl, and he will then serve him forever.

Question: Irrelevant Topic!

TEXT 2

SHEMOT (EXODUS) 12:35–36

> וּבְנֵי יִשְׂרָאֵל עָשׂוּ כִּדְבַר מֹשֶׁה, וַיִּשְׁאֲלוּ מִמִּצְרַיִם כְּלֵי כֶסֶף וּכְלֵי זָהָב וּשְׂמָלֹת:
>
> וַה' נָתַן אֶת חֵן הָעָם בְּעֵינֵי מִצְרַיִם, וַיַּשְׁאִלוּם, וַיְנַצְּלוּ אֶת מִצְרָיִם:

And the Children of Israel fulfilled Moses's instruction and borrowed from the Egyptians silver objects, golden objects, and garments. G-d gave the people favor in the eyes of the Egyptians, and the [Egyptians] lent them, and the [Jews] emptied out Egypt.

TEXT 3

MIDRASH TANCHUMA, BESHALACH 16

> בשעה שיצאו ישראל ממצרים, יצא פרעה לרדוף אותם . . . עמד וקישט כל אותם הסוסים באבנים טובות ומרגליות. כשבאו לים וטבען הקדוש ברוך הוא, היו צפין על שפת הים כל אותן אבנים טובות ומרגליות, והיו מושלכים. והיו ישראל יורדין בכל יום ונוטלין מהם.

When the Jewish people left Egypt, Pharaoh pursued them. . . . [Pharaoh] adorned his army's horses with diamonds and gems. When they reached the Red Sea and drowned, all the diamonds and gems rose to the surface and washed up on shore, where they lay abandoned. For days, the Jews made their way to shore and collected the valuables.

Tanchuma

A Midrashic work bearing the name of Rabbi Tanchuma, a 4th-century Talmudic sage quoted often in this work. "Midrash" is the designation of a particular genre of rabbinic literature usually forming a running commentary on specific books of the Bible. *Tanchuma* provides textual exegeses, expounds upon the biblical narrative, and develops and illustrates moral principles. *Tanchuma* is unique in that many of its sections commence with a halachic discussion, which subsequently leads into nonhalachic teachings.

TEXT 4

JERUSALEM TALMUD TRACTATE ROSH HASHANAH 17A

אמר רב שמואל אמר רב יצחק: "וידבר ה' אל משה ואל אהרן, ויצום אל
בני ישראל". על מה ציוום?

על שילוח עבדים.

Jerusalem Talmud

A commentary to the Mishnah, compiled during the 4th and 5th centuries. The Jerusalem Talmud predates its Babylonian counterpart by 100 years and is written in both Hebrew and Aramaic. While the Babylonian Talmud is the most authoritative source for Jewish law, the Jerusalem Talmud remains an invaluable source for the spiritual, intellectual, ethical, historical, and legal traditions of Judaism.

Rabbi Shmuel, the son of Rabbi Yitzchak, said, "Which commandment does the passage refer to when it reads, 'And G-d spoke to Moses and Aaron and instructed them about the Children of Israel'?"

It was about the mitzvah to liberate their slaves.

TEXT 5

YIRMIYAHU (JEREMIAH) 34:12–14

וַיְהִי דְבַר ה' אֶל יִרְמְיָהוּ, מֵאֵת ה' לֵאמֹר:

כֹּה אָמַר ה' אֱלֹקֵי יִשְׂרָאֵל, אָנֹכִי כָּרַתִּי בְרִית אֶת אֲבוֹתֵיכֶם, בְּיוֹם הוֹצִאִי
אוֹתָם מֵאֶרֶץ מִצְרַיִם מִבֵּית עֲבָדִים, לֵאמֹר:

מִקֵּץ שֶׁבַע שָׁנִים, תְּשַׁלְּחוּ אִישׁ אֶת אָחִיו הָעִבְרִי אֲשֶׁר יִמָּכֵר לְךָ וַעֲבָדְךָ
שֵׁשׁ שָׁנִים, וְשִׁלַּחְתּוֹ חָפְשִׁי מֵעִמָּךְ:

The word of G-d came to Jeremiah, saying,

"So says the G-d of Israel: I made a covenant with your fathers on the day that I brought them out of the land of Egypt, out of the house of slaves, saying,

"'Every man, at the end of seven years, release your Jewish brother who has been sold to you; when he has served you for six years, give him his freedom.'"

II. THREE ANSWERS

1. *Importance Linked with Creation*

TEXT 6

NACHMANIDES, EXODUS 21:2

> התחיל המשפט הראשון בעבד עברי, מפני שיש בשילוח העבד בשנה
> השביעית זכר ליציאת מצרים, הנזכר בדיבור הראשון . . . ויש בה עוד
> זכר למעשה בראשית כשבת, כי השנה השביעית לעבד – שבתון
> ממלאכת אדוניו, כיום השביעי. ויש בה עוד שביעי בשנים שהוא
> היובל, כי השביעי נבחר בימים, בשנים וביובל, והכל לענין אחד . . .
> ולכן המצוה הזאת ראויה להקדים אותה, שהיא נכבדת מאוד, רומזת
> דברים גדולים במעשה בראשית.

Rabbi Moshe ben Nachman (Nachmanides, Ramban)
1194–1270

Scholar, philosopher, author, and physician. Nachmanides was born in Spain and served as leader of Iberian Jewry. In 1263, he was summoned by King James of Aragon to a public disputation with Pablo Cristiani, a Jewish apostate. Though Nachmanides was the clear victor of the debate, he had to flee Spain because of the resulting persecution. He moved to Israel and helped reestablish communal life in Jerusalem. He authored a classic commentary on the Pentateuch and a commentary on the Talmud.

The Torah begins with the commandment concerning the Jewish slave because the slave's liberation in the seventh year is reminiscent of our liberation from Egypt, mentioned in the first of the Ten Commandments. . . . It is also reminiscent of Creation, as is the Sabbath, since the slave's seventh year is like a Sabbath of sorts—it is when he is freed from serving his master. The slave has an additional liberation date in the Jubilee (the year that follows the seventh set of seven years) because the seventh was selected by G-d to represent freedom in terms of days, years, and the Jubilee. Thus, because of their distinction and because the laws of slavery parallel important themes of Creation, they were chosen as the introductory mitzvah.

2. Slaves: Never Again!

TEXT 7

RABBI ABRAHAM IBN EZRA, EXODUS 21:2

ואין לאדם יותר קשה עליו, מהיותו ברשות אדם כמוהו. על כן החל
משפט העבד.

There is nothing more difficult in the human experience than to be bonded to a fellow human; therefore, the Torah begins with the laws of slavery.

Rabbi Abraham ibn Ezra
1092–1167

Biblical commentator, linguist, and poet. Ibn Ezra was born in Toledo, Spain, and fled the Almohad regime to other parts of Europe. It is believed that he was living in London at the time of his death. Ibn Ezra is best known for his literalistic commentary on the Pentateuch. He also wrote works of poetry, philosophy, medicine, astronomy, and other topics.

3. Unpacking the Generals

TEXT 8

RABBI DON ISAAC ABARBANEL, EXODUS 21:2

הקדוש ברוך הוא השמיע לעמו עשרת הדיברות מאמרים קצרים,
וכאשר ישראל לא רצו לשמוע מפי הגבורה התולדות ותולדות
התולדות מהדיבורים ההם . . . הוצרך יתברך לצוות את משה שישים
לפניהם אלה המשפטים . . . כי הם באמת ציווים נכללים בעשרת
הדיברות. ולזה אמר "ואלה המשפטים אשר תשים לפניהם" בוא"ו
העטוף, כלומר: שים לפניהם הדברים שנכללו בדיברות אשר שמעו . . .
כי הנה החכם יודע כי כל המשפטים האלו נכללו בדיברות ההם, ויותר
מהמה גם כן, אבל הספיק בזכרון אלה שיבואו בפרשה לביאור כוונתו,
והוא הבין למצות אחרות שיזכור אחר זה.

Rabbi Don Isaac Abarbanel
1437–1508

Biblical exegete and statesman.
Abarbanel was born in Lisbon, Portugal,
and served as a minister in the court
of King Alfonso V of Portugal. After
intrigues at court led to accusations
against him, he fled to Spain, where
he once again served as a counselor
to royalty. It is claimed that Abarbanel
offered King Ferdinand and Queen
Isabella large sums of money for the
revocation of their Edict of Expulsion of
1492, but to no avail. After the expulsion,
he eventually settled in Italy, where
he wrote a commentary on Scripture,
as well as other venerated works.

G-d gave his nation ten brief commandments, but since they were unable to hear the subsets of these commandments . . . G-d had to instruct Moses to teach them these laws . . . which are clear subsets of the Ten Commandments. He therefore opened with the words "and these are the laws that you should place before them." And implies that these laws are [a continuation of the Ten Commandments because they are] included in those commandments. . . . A wise person knows that all these laws and more are contained in the commandments. However, G-d illustrated His point with these laws and left the wise person to infer that the same applies to all the laws that the Torah would eventually elucidate.

Commandment	Sub Law	Rationale
Murder	Slavery	Slavery is like a living death.
	Injuring a Parent	Inflicting an open wound on a parent is the equivalent of murder.
	Cursing a Parent	Committing murder with words
	Kidnapping	Deprives the victim's parents of life
	Killing a Slave	Is an actual murder
	Your Ox Gores a Person	Your possessions cause the murder of a fellow human.

TEXT 9

TALMUD, KIDUSHIN 22B

רבן יוחנן בן זכאי היה דורש את המקרא הזה כמין חומר: מה נשתנה
אוזן מכל איברים שבגוף? אמר הקדוש ברוך הוא: אוזן ששמעה קולי
על הר סיני בשעה שאמרתי: "כי לי בני ישראל עבדים" (ויקרא כה, נה),
ולא עבדים לעבדים, והלך זה וקנה אדון לעצמו – יירצע.

Rabban Jochanan ben Zakkai would interpret this verse in a beautiful manner. Why was the ear singled out from all the limbs in the body? G-d said, on Mount Sinai, "The ear heard me proclaim, 'For the Children of Israel are My slaves,' not slaves of slaves. Then this person went and acquired a master for himself? Let his ear be pierced."

Babylonian Talmud

A literary work of monumental proportions that draws upon the legal, spiritual, intellectual, ethical, and historical traditions of Judaism. The 37 tractates of the Babylonian Talmud contain the teachings of the Jewish sages from the period after the destruction of the 2nd Temple through the 5th century CE. It has served as the primary vehicle for the transmission of the Oral Law and the education of Jews over the centuries; it is the entry point for all subsequent legal, ethical, and theological Jewish scholarship.

Introduction to the Entire Torah: It's a Part of You

TEXT 10

THE REBBE, RABBI MENACHEM MENDEL SCHNEERSON, LIKUTEI SICHOT 16, P. 256

בא אנדערע מצות געפינט מען ניט אז די תורה זאל מדגיש זיין די שייכות פון דעם שכר מצוה צו דער מצוה. ובדוגמא: די מצוה פון כיבוד אב ואם, וואס איר שכר איז "למען יאריכון ימיך" (שמות כא, ה) . . . איז אין דעם מהות השכר ניט קענטיק די שייכות צו דער מצוה דוקא.

ועל דרך זה ביי עונשים אויף עבירות, זעט מען ניט אין דעם עונש . . . א באזונדערע שייכות צו די עבירות, וואס זיינען מחייב די עונשין.

ביי עבד עברי אבער פארבינדט די תורה דעם עונש מיט זיין סיבה: "ורצע וגו' את אזנו" קומט דערפאר וואס "אוזן ששמעה על הר סיני כו'" . . .

דערמיט איז מבואר וואס "כי תקנה עבד עברי" (שמות כא, א) איז דער ערשטער פון די משפטים וואס די תורה זאגט אן תיכף לאחר מתן תורה בהר סיני: בא אן עבד עברי זעט זיך אן (אין זיין עונש) באופן גלוי וניכר (אויך אין זיין גוף הגשמי) דער פארבונד פון זיין משפט מיט "הר סיני".

Rabbi Menachem Mendel Schneerson
1902–1994

The towering Jewish leader of the 20th century, known as "the Lubavitcher Rebbe," or simply as "the Rebbe." Born in southern Ukraine, the Rebbe escaped Nazi-occupied Europe, arriving in the U.S. in June 1941. The Rebbe inspired and guided the revival of traditional Judaism after the European devastation, impacting virtually every Jewish community the world over. The Rebbe often emphasized that the performance of just one additional good deed could usher in the era of Mashiach. The Rebbe's scholarly talks and writings have been printed in more than 200 volumes.

The Torah does not usually emphasize a link between the reward of a mitzvah and the mitzvah. For example, the reward for honoring a parent is longevity, but there is no obvious link between longevity and honoring a parent. The same is true of sins. We don't see specific links between the sins and the punishments that they incur. The laws of slavery are different. In this instance, the Torah links the punishment with what caused it. The ear is pierced because it is the limb that heard G-d say on Mount Sinai that Jews can only be enslaved to G-d.

This helps us understand why the laws of slavery were the first to be taught after G-d gave us the Torah on Mount Sinai. In [the punishment for] this law, we see a clear and obvious link [one that is manifested in the physical body] between the law and Mount Sinai.

7.

Terumah

The Timeless Temple

Bringing the Message of the Temple to Every Corner of Life

Dedicated in loving memory of Rabbi Daniel Moscowitz,
הרה"ח השליח ר' דניאל יצחק ע"ה בן יבלחט"א ר' אפרים שיחי',
Regional Director of Chabad of Illinois, marking his yahrtzeit on 2 Adar.

May the merit of the Torah study worldwide accompany his soul in the world of everlasting life and be a source of blessings to his family with much health, happiness, nachas, and success.

PARSHA OVERVIEW

Terumah

The people of Israel are called upon to contribute thirteen materials—gold, silver, and copper; blue-, purple-, and red-dyed wool; flax, goat hair, animal skins, wood, olive oil, spices, and gems—out of which, G-d says to Moses, "They shall make for Me a Sanctuary, and I shall dwell amidst them."

On the summit of Mount Sinai, Moses is given detailed instructions on how to construct this dwelling for G-d so that it could be readily dismantled, transported, and reassembled as the people journeyed in the desert.

In the Sanctuary's inner chamber, behind an artistically woven curtain, was the ark containing the Tablets of Testimony engraved with the Ten Commandments; on the ark's cover stood two winged cherubim hammered out of pure gold. In the outer chamber stood the seven-branched *menorah* and the table upon which the "showbread" was arranged.

The Sanctuary's three walls were fitted together from forty-eight upright wooden boards, each of which was overlaid with gold and held up by a pair of silver foundation sockets. The roof was formed of three layers of coverings: (a) tapestries of multicolored wool and linen, (b) a covering made of goat hair, and (c) a covering of ram and *tachash* skins. Across the front of the Sanctuary was an embroidered screen held up by five posts.

Surrounding the Sanctuary and the copper-plated altar that stood before it was an enclosure of linen hangings, supported by sixty wooden posts with silver hooks and trimmings, and reinforced by copper stakes.

I. THE MISHKAN'S CONSTRUCTION

The Capital Campaign

TEXT 1

SHEMOT (EXODUS) 25:1-9

וַיְדַבֵּר ה' אֶל מֹשֶׁה לֵּאמֹר:

דַּבֵּר אֶל בְּנֵי יִשְׂרָאֵל, וְיִקְחוּ לִי תְּרוּמָה, מֵאֵת כָּל אִישׁ אֲשֶׁר יִדְּבֶנּוּ לִבּוֹ תִּקְחוּ אֶת תְּרוּמָתִי:

וְזֹאת הַתְּרוּמָה אֲשֶׁר תִּקְחוּ מֵאִתָּם, זָהָב וָכֶסֶף וּנְחֹשֶׁת:

וּתְכֵלֶת וְאַרְגָּמָן וְתוֹלַעַת שָׁנִי וְשֵׁשׁ וְעִזִּים:

וְעֹרֹת אֵילִם מְאָדָּמִים וְעֹרֹת תְּחָשִׁים וַעֲצֵי שִׁטִּים:

שֶׁמֶן לַמָּאוֹר, בְּשָׂמִים לְשֶׁמֶן הַמִּשְׁחָה וְלִקְטֹרֶת הַסַּמִּים:

אַבְנֵי שֹׁהַם וְאַבְנֵי מִלֻּאִים, לָאֵפֹד וְלַחֹשֶׁן:

וְעָשׂוּ לִי מִקְדָּשׁ, וְשָׁכַנְתִּי בְּתוֹכָם:

כְּכֹל אֲשֶׁר אֲנִי מַרְאֶה אוֹתְךָ, אֵת תַּבְנִית הַמִּשְׁכָּן וְאֵת תַּבְנִית כָּל כֵּלָיו, וְכֵן תַּעֲשׂוּ:

G-d spoke to Moses, saying:

"Speak to the Children of Israel, and have them take for Me an offering; from every person whose heart inspires him to generosity, you shall take My offering.

"And this is the offering that you shall take from them: gold, silver, and copper.

"Blue, purple, and crimson wool; linen and goat hair.

"Ram skins dyed red, *tachash* skins, and acacia wood.

"Oil for lighting, spices for the anointing oil and for the incense.

"*Shoham* stones and filling stones for the ephod and for the *choshen*.

"And they shall make Me a sanctuary, and I will dwell in their midst.

"According to all that I show you, the pattern of the Mishkan and the pattern of all its vessels; and so shall you do."

Four Materials, Four Kingdoms

TEXT 2

MIDRASH TANCHUMA, TERUMAH 7

זהב – כנגד מלכות בבל, דכתיב ביה: אנת הוא ראשה די דהבא.

כסף – כנגד מלכות מדי, דכתיב: "ועשרת אלפים ככר כסף".

נחושת – כנגד מלכות יון, שהיא פחותה מכולם.

ועורות אלים מאדמים – כנגד מלכות אדום, שנאמר: "ויצא הראשון אדמוני".

אמר הקדוש ברוך הוא: אף על פי שאתם רואין ארבע מלכויות מתגאות ובאות עליכם, אני מצמיח לכם ישועה מתוך שיעבוד.

Tanchuma

A Midrashic work bearing the name of Rabbi Tanchuma, a 4th-century Talmudic sage quoted often in this work. "Midrash" is the designation of a particular genre of rabbinic literature usually forming a running commentary on specific books of the Bible. *Tanchuma* provides textual exegeses, expounds upon the biblical narrative, and develops and illustrates moral principles. *Tanchuma* is unique in that many of its sections commence with a halachic discussion, which subsequently leads into nonhalachic teachings.

The gold [used in the Tabernacle] corresponds to the kingdom of Babylonia, of which the verse states, "You are the head of gold."

The silver corresponds to the kingdom of Media [Persia], as the verse states, "[If it pleases the king, let it be written to destroy them,] and I will weigh out ten thousand silver talents. . . ."

The copper corresponds to the kingdom of Greece, as it was the least powerful of them all.

And the red-dyed ram skins correspond to the kingdom of Edom, as the verse states, "And the first one emerged reddish. . . ."

G-d said, "Though you witness four kingdoms boastfully dominating you, I will sow salvation for you from the midst of your servitude."

Why Ruin the Party?

TEXT 3

THE REBBE, RABBI MENACHEM MENDEL SCHNEERSON, LIKUTEI SICHOT 16, P. 293

> איז תמוה ביותר: וואס פאר א קשר ושייכות איז דא צווישן ד' מלכיות
> און תרומת המשכן? אדרבא – די ד' מלכיות האבן דאך געבראכט די ד'
> גליות און דעם חורבן בית המקדש, וואס דאס איז דער היפך פון תרומת
> המשכן, וואס ענינה איז – ועשו לי מקדש (בנין והקמת המשכן)?

It is baffling: What do the four kingdoms have to do with the donations for the Tabernacle? Moreover: the "four kingdoms" precipitated the "four Exiles" and the *destruction* of the Temple, the very opposite of the donations, which were intended to *build* the Tabernacle.

Rabbi Menachem Mendel Schneerson
1902–1994

The towering Jewish leader of the 20th century, known as "the Lubavitcher Rebbe," or simply as "the Rebbe." Born in southern Ukraine, the Rebbe escaped Nazi-occupied Europe, arriving in the U.S. in June 1941. The Rebbe inspired and guided the revival of traditional Judaism after the European devastation, impacting virtually every Jewish community the world over. The Rebbe often emphasized that the performance of just one additional good deed could usher in the era of Mashiach. The Rebbe's scholarly talks and writings have been printed in more than 200 volumes.

II. TORAH, PRAYER, AND *MITZVOT*

Three Campaigns

TEXT 4

RASHI, SHEMOT (EXODUS) 25:2

"תקחו את תרומתי": אמרו רבותינו: שלוש תרומות אמורות כאן, אחת, תרומה בקע לגולגולת, שנעשו מהם האדנים . . . ואחת, תרומת המזבח – בקע לגולגולת לקופות, לקנות מהן קרבנות צבור. ואחת, תרומת המשכן, נדבת כל אחד ואחד. שלושה עשר דברים האמורים בענין, כולם הוצרכו למלאכת המשכן או לבגדי כהונה, כשתדקדק בהם.

Rabbi Shlomo Yitzchaki (Rashi)
1040–1105

Most noted biblical and Talmudic commentator. Born in Troyes, France, Rashi studied in the famed *yeshivot* of Mainz and Worms. His commentaries on the Pentateuch and the Talmud, which focus on the straightforward meaning of the text, appear in virtually every edition of the Talmud and Bible.

"You shall take My offering." Our rabbis said: [The word *terumah* (offering) is mentioned three times, indicating that] three offerings are mentioned here:

One is the offering of a half-shekel per head, from which they made the sockets. . . . Another is the offering of a half-shekel per head for the [community] coffers, from which to purchase the communal sacrifices, and another is the offering for the Tabernacle, each individual's donation.

The thirteen materials mentioned in this section were all required for the work of the Mishkan or for the garments of the priests, as you will find when you study them closely.

On Three Things the World Stands

TEXT 5

PIRKEI AVOT (ETHICS OF THE FATHERS) 1:2

Ethics of the Fathers
(*Pirkei Avot*)

A 6-chapter work on Jewish ethics that is studied widely by Jewish communities, especially during the summer. The first 5 chapters are from the Mishnah, tractate Avot. Avot differs from the rest of the Mishnah in that it does not focus on legal subjects; it is a collection of the sages' wisdom on topics related to character development, ethics, healthy living, piety, and the study of Torah.

שִׁמְעוֹן הַצַּדִּיק הָיָה מִשְּׁיָרֵי כְנֶסֶת הַגְּדוֹלָה. הוּא הָיָה אוֹמֵר: עַל שְׁלֹשָׁה דְבָרִים הָעוֹלָם עוֹמֵד: עַל הַתּוֹרָה, וְעַל הָעֲבוֹדָה, וְעַל גְּמִילוּת חֲסָדִים.

Shimon the Righteous was among the last surviving members of the Great Assembly. He would say, "The world stands on three things: Torah, the service of G-d, and kind deeds."

Three Collections for Three Components of Life

TEXT 6

THE REBBE, RABBI MENACHEM MENDEL SCHNEERSON,
LIKUTEI SICHOT 16, PP. 293–294

> . . . "תורה" (פון עמוד דער) איז 'ה עבודת ענייני אלע פון יסוד דער
> אנהויב און מקור זיין האט המצוות קיום און אידישקייט פון ענין יעדער
> דער זיינען זיי וואס האדנים, תרומת אין מרומז איז דאס – תורה אין
> משכן. פון יסוד
>
> איז ציבור, קרבנות געקויפט מ'האט וועלכער פון השקלים, תרומת
> תפילה און הקרבנות, עבודת איז דאס (וואס "עבודה" פון קו דער
> תקנום); קרבנות שבמקום
>
> (זהב גשמיים דברים אלע די ארום נעמט וואס המשכן, תרומת און
> כנגד איז משכן, דעם געבויט מ'האט וועלכע פון וגו') ונחושת וכסף
> און וגו') זהב דורך מקיים מ'איז (וועלכע מצוות פון עבודה דער
> איז חסדים גמילות אז [כידוע, חסדים גמילות איז כללותם וואס
> המצוות"]. "כללות

The first step to serving G-d is (the pillar of) "Torah." . . . Every facet of Judaism and the *mitzvot* have their source in the Torah—alluded to by the donations for the sockets, the foundation of the Tabernacle.

As for the half-shekel donations used to purchase communal offerings, they represent the pillar of "service," namely, the sacrificial services, and in the present day, the service of prayer.

The donations of various materials used in the Tabernacle's construction (gold, silver, and copper, etc.) represent the performance of the various *mitzvot* (which are fulfilled with various physical materials such as gold, etc.), and which generally are embodied by deeds of kindness [for kind deeds are considered the "embodiment of the *mitzvot*"].

Torah: Exercise of the Mind

TEXT 7

RABBI SHNEUR ZALMAN OF LIADI, TANYA, CHAPTER 5

הנה כל שכל, כשמשכיל ומשיג בשכלו איזה מושכל – הרי השכל
תופס את המושכל, ומקיפו בשכלו. והמושכל, נתפס ומוקף ומלובש
בתוך השכל שהשיגו והשכילו. וגם השכל מלובש במושכל, בשעה
שמשיגו ותופסו בשכלו. דרך משל – כשאדם מבין ומשיג איזו הלכה
במשנה או בגמרא לאשורה על בוריה, הרי שכלו תופס ומקיף אותה,
וגם שכלו מלובש בה באותה שעה. והנה הלכה זו – היא חכמתו ורצונו
של הקדוש ברוך הוא... הרי כשהאדם יודע ומשיג בשכלו פסק... הרי
זה משיג ותופס ומקיף בשכלו רצונו וחכמתו של הקדוש ברוך הוא,
דלית מחשבה תפיסא ביה. ולא ברצונו וחכמתו, כי אם בהתלבשותם
בהלכות הערוכות לפנינו, וגם שכלו מלובש בהם. והוא יחוד נפלא
שאין יחוד כמוהו, ולא כערכו נמצא כלל בגשמיות – להיות לאחדים
ומיוחדים ממש, מכל צד ופנה.

**Rabbi Shneur Zalman of Liadi
(Alter Rebbe)**
1745–1812

Chasidic rebbe, halachic authority, and
founder of the Chabad movement.
The Alter Rebbe was born in Liozna,
Belarus, and was among the principal
students of the Magid of Mezeritch.
His numerous works include the
Tanya, an early classic containing the
fundamentals of Chabad Chasidism;
and *Shulchan Aruch HaRav*, an expanded
and reworked code of Jewish law.

When the mind conceives and comprehends a concept with its intellectual faculties, it grasps the concept and encompasses it, so that the concept is contained . . . within the mind. . . . The mind, for its part, is also surrounded by the concept. . . . For example, when a person understands a halachah in the Mishnah or Talmud fully and clearly, his mind encompasses and grasps it, while simultaneously being encompassed by it.

Now, halachah is the wisdom and will of G-d . . . so when a person's mind masters it . . . he is grasping the will and wisdom of the Holy One, blessed be He, Whom no thought can grasp, nor His will and wisdom, except when they are contained in the laws that have been set out for us. [Simultaneously,] his mind is encompassed by [the divine will and wisdom].

This is a wonderful union, like which there is none other, and without parallel anywhere in the material world, a union of complete oneness from every side and angle.

Prayer: Exercise of the Heart

TEXT 8

TALMUD TRACTATE TAANIT, 2A

> "לאהבה את ה' אלקיכם ולעבדו בכל לבבכם". איזו היא עבודה שהיא
> בלב? הוי אומר, זו תפילה.

The verse states, "To love the L-rd your G-d and to serve Him with all your heart." Which is the service of G-d that is performed in the heart? It refers to prayer.

Mitzvot: *Exercise of the Body*

TEXT 9

THE REBBE, RABBI MENACHEM MENDEL SCHNEERSON, LIKUTEI SICHOT 16, P. 295

> אין . . . תורה ועבודה – איז דא א צד השווה, אז ביי זיי ביידע איז די
> התעסקות פון אדם העובד אין און מיט זיך . . . און דאס איז דער יתרון
> אין דעם דריטן קו – גמילות חסדים, וואס איז כולל קיום כל המצוות –
> צו אויפטאן (בעיקר) אין דעם דבר גשמי (מיט וועלכן מ'איז מקיים די
> מצוה), אז אזוי ווי ער איז (בחיצוניות) אין זיין ציור פון דברים תחתונים
> גשמיים, אין זיין "גשמיות", זאל ער ווערן א חפץ של מצוה.

Babylonian Talmud

A literary work of monumental proportions that draws upon the legal, spiritual, intellectual, ethical, and historical traditions of Judaism. The 37 tractates of the Babylonian Talmud contain the teachings of the Jewish sages from the period after the destruction of the 2nd Temple through the 5th century CE. It has served as the primary vehicle for the transmission of the Oral Law and the education of Jews over the centuries; it is the entry point for all subsequent legal, ethical, and theological Jewish scholarship.

Torah study and prayer both involve an experience that takes place *within* a person. . . . [By contrast,] the third pillar—kind deeds, which includes all the *mitzvot*—is unique in that it [doesn't take place within a person, but rather] involves physical objects (used in *mitzvot*), so that something, even as it remains a physical object, can become [as holy as] the object of a *mitzvah*.

III. THE EXPERIENCE VS. THE GOAL

The Lowliest Place

Question for Discussion

Which category would you say is more central to Jewish life and the Jewish role in this world: the spiritual experience of Torah/prayer or the (sometimes apparently prosaic) rituals?

TEXT **10**

RABBI SHNEUR ZALMAN OF LIADI, TANYA, CHAPTER 36

> והנה מודעת זאת מאמר רבותנו זכרונם לברכה, שתכלית בריאת עולם
> הזה הוא, שנתאוה הקדוש ברוך הוא להיות לו דירה בתחתונים . . .
> עד שנברא עולם הזה הגשמי והחומרי ממש, והוא התחתון במדרגה,
> שאין תחתון למטה ממנו, בענין הסתר אורו יתברך. וחושך כפול
> ומכופל, עד שהוא מלא קליפות וסטרא אחרא שהן נגד ה' ממש, לומר
> אני ואפסי עוד.

We know from our sages that the purpose behind the creation of this world is G-d's desire for a home in the lowest realms.... Thus, this tangibly physical world was created; it is the lowest realm. There is no place where G-d is so hidden, and that is so dark, full of *kelipot* that literally oppose G-d, declaring, "I, and nothing else, exists!"

Action Is Great

TEXT 11

TALMUD TRACTATE KIDUSHIN, 40B

וכבר היה רבי טרפון וזקנים מסובין בעלית בית נתזה בלוד, ונשאלה
שאלה זו בפניהם: תלמוד גדול, או מעשה גדול? נענה רבי טרפון ואמר:
מעשה גדול. נענה רבי עקיבא ואמר: תלמוד גדול. נענו כולם ואמרו:
תלמוד גדול, שהתלמוד מביא לידי מעשה.

There was an incident in which Rabbi Tarfon and the Elders were reclining in the loft of the house of Nitza in Lod, when this question was asked of them: Is Torah study greater or is action [i.e., performing *mitzvot*] greater?

Rabbi Tarfon answered and said, "Action is greater."

Rabbi Akiva answered and said, "Torah study is greater."

Everyone answered and said, "Torah study is greater, because Torah study leads to action."

The Main Thing

TEXT 12

THE REBBE, RABBI MENACHEM MENDEL SCHNEERSON, LIKUTEI SICHOT 16, P. 297

. . . וואָס די תורה רעדט בפירוש אין אונזער פרשה נאָר וועגן תרומת
המשכן, ווײַל דאָס איז דער עיקר ותכלית הכוונה; און די אַנדערע צוויי
תרומות ווערן דערמאָנט נאָר בכלל ובדרך רמז, ווײַל זיי זײַנען (בהכוונה
העיקרית) בלויז א הכנה והקדמה (והשלמה) צו דער עשיית הדירה.

The only one [of the three collections] mentioned explicitly in the *parsha* is the collection of materials for the Tabernacle's construction [which represent the *mitzvot*]—because that's the most important thing. The other collections [which represent Torah study and prayer] are alluded in passing only, because (at their core) they are simply the groundwork that makes the construction (and function) of [G-d's home] possible.

A Global Mission

TEXT **13**

THE REBBE, RABBI MENACHEM MENDEL SCHNEERSON, IBID.

און דאס איז אויך דער ביאור אין דברי המדרש הנזכר לעיל . . . אז
"זהב וכסף וגו'" זיינען כנגד די ד' מלכיות:

וויבאלד אז דער ענין פון תרומת המשכן איז צו מאכן א דירה לו יתברך
בתחתונים (פון די דברים גשמיים מאכן א מקדש ומשכן לה') – איז
די שלימות פון דעם ענין (ניט אזוי אין בנין המשכן, אין וועלכן מ'האט
געזען בעיני בשר ווי אין זיי איז דא השראת השכינה, נאר) אין דער
עבודה בזמן הגלות, וען גשמיות העולם איז בתקפו, און דורך דער
עבודה צו איבערמאכן אויך אט דעם גשם, איז מען מברר דעם תחתון
"שאין תחתון למטה ממנו".

This explains the idea in the Midrash that the "gold and silver,
etc.," of the Tabernacle correspond to the "four kingdoms":

The purpose of the donated materials was to build a home for
G-d in this world. . . . This is most fully accomplished (not so
much by building the physical Tabernacle, a place of overt spiri-
tuality, but) by our efforts during the Exile—an era gripped by
the physical trappings of the world. By our efforts to transform
this degree of brute materialism [to holiness], we uplift the most
crass elements of the physical reality.

Just to Do a Favor for Another

TEXT 14

THE REBBE, RABBI MENACHEM MENDEL SCHNEERSON, HAYOM YOM, 5 IYAR

רבינו הזקן קבל מר' מרדכי הצדיק ששמע מהבעל שם טוב: עס קומט
אראפ א נשמה אויף דער וועלט, און לעבט אפ זיבעציג אכציג יאהר,
צוליב טאן א אידען א טובה בגשמיות ובפרט אין רוחניות.

The Alter Rebbe received the following teaching from the *tzadik* Reb Mordechai, who had heard it from the Baal Shem Tov: a soul may descend to this world and live seventy or eighty years in order to do a Jew a material favor, and certainly a spiritual one.

Hayom Yom

In 1942, Rabbi Yosef Yitzchak Schneersohn, the 6th Rebbe of Chabad, gave his son-in-law, the future Rebbe, the task of compiling an anthology of Chasidic aphorisms and customs arranged according to the days of the year. In describing the completed product, Rabbi Yosef YitZchak wrote that it is "a book that is small in format but bursting with pearls and diamonds of the choicest quality."

A Real Education

TEXT 15

RABBI HILLEL ZALTZMAN, SAMARKAND (BROOKLYN, N.Y.: CHAMAH, 2015), P. 32

Once, during a Hebrew writing lesson, my friend Mordechai Goldschmidt forgot his inkwell. I didn't want to let him dip his pen into my inkwell, and told him that he should have brought his own. Reb Bentcha noticed this, but said nothing.

After a while he asked me, "Hilke, did you say *Modeh Ani* today?" *Modeh Ani* is the first prayer of the day, an acknowledgement of G-d recited immediately upon waking up each morning. I said that I had.

Reb Bentcha asked me to explain the *Modeh Ani*, which I did to the best of my ability. Reb Bentcha stopped me and in the manner he reserved for chastising someone, said disapprovingly, "That's not what it means," and he went on to explain it:

"*Modeh* means selflessness. This means that when a friend asks for ink, you give it to him. *Ani* means that when your friend asks you for a pen, you must give him a pen," and so he went on to explain the rest of the words in a similar fashion. "Now do you know the meaning of *Modeh Ani*?" he concluded.

These scenes typified his method of education, and they have remained etched in our souls for life.

8.

Purim

It's a Different World Today.
It's Time to Play Offense.

Asserting Our Judaism in a Society Ready to Hear Our Message

Dedicated in loving memory of Mrs. Golda Mindel Grossman,
גאלדא מינדל בת שרה ע"ה, *marking her yahrtzeit on 10 Adar I.*

*May the merit of the Torah study worldwide accompany her soul in the
world of everlasting life and be a source of blessings to her family with
much health, happiness, nachas, and success.*

HOLIDAY OVERVIEW

Purim

The jolly festival of Purim is celebrated every year on the fourteenth day of the Hebrew month of Adar (late winter/ early spring). It commemorates the salvation of the Jewish people in ancient Persia from Haman's plot "to destroy, kill, and annihilate all the Jews, young and old, infants and women, in a single day," as recorded in the *Megillah* (biblical book of Esther).

The Persian Empire of the fourth century BCE extended over 127 lands, and all the Jews were its subjects. When King Ahasuerus had his wife, Queen Vashti, executed for failing to follow his orders, he arranged a beauty pageant to find a new queen. A Jewish girl, Esther, found favor in his eyes and became the new queen, though she refused to divulge her nationality.

Meanwhile, the Jew-hating Haman was appointed prime minister of the empire. Mordecai, the leader of the Jews (and Esther's cousin), defied the king's orders and refused to bow to Haman. Haman was incensed, and he convinced the king to issue a decree ordering the extermination of all the Jews on the thirteenth day of Adar, a date chosen by a lottery Haman made.

Mordecai galvanized all the Jews, convincing them to repent, fast, and pray to G-d. Meanwhile, Esther asked the king and Haman to join her for a feast. At a subsequent feast, Esther revealed to the king her Jewish identity. Haman was hanged, Mordecai was appointed prime minister in his stead, and a new decree was issued, granting the Jews the right to defend themselves against their enemies.

On the thirteenth of Adar, the Jews mobilized and killed many of their enemies. On the fourteenth of Adar, they rested and celebrated. In the capital city of Shushan, they took one more day to finish the job.

I. NAVIGATION ISSUES

For the Record

TEXT 1

RABBI YAAKOV MOSHE LORBERBAUM, MEGILAT SETARIM 9:29

> ונראה דמרדכי לא ציווה רק על עשיית השמחה בימי הפורים, אבל
> כתיבת וקריאת המגילה – היתה רק אסתר העיקר, כמבואר במסכת
> מגילה, ששלחה אסתר לחכמים "כתבוני לדורות", ומצאו לה מקרא.

Rabbi Yaakov Lorberbaum of Lissa
1770–1832

Rabbi and halachic authority. A scion of a distinguished line of rabbis, Rabbi Lorberbaum served as the rabbi of Lissa, Poland. He was a prolific author who wrote commentaries to many books of the Bible and works of original analysis covering all areas of Jewish law. Rabbi Lorberbaum is best known for *Chavat Daat*, about matters of ritual law, and *Netivot Hamishpat*, concerning tort law.

The verses imply that Mordecai only called for Purim to be commemorated with joy, but he did not call for its documentation nor its annual public reading. It was Esther who primarily pushed for this, as the Talmud relates, "Esther sent to the sages, 'Write my story for future generations.'"

Brought to Their Knees

TEXT 2

TALMUD TRACTATE MEGILLAH, 12A

שאלו תלמידיו את רבי שמעון בר יוחאי: מפני מה נתחייבו שונאיהן
של ישראל שבאותו הדור כליה?

אמר להם: אמרו אתם.

אמרו לו: מפני שנהנו מסעודתו של אותו רשע.

אם כן – שבשושן יהרגו, שבכל העולם כולו אל יהרגו!

אמרו לו: אמור אתה.

אמר להם: מפני שהשתחוו לצלם.

Babylonian Talmud

A literary work of monumental proportions that draws upon the legal, spiritual, intellectual, ethical, and historical traditions of Judaism. The 37 tractates of the Babylonian Talmud contain the teachings of the Jewish sages from the period after the destruction of the 2nd Temple through the 5th century CE. It has served as the primary vehicle for the transmission of the Oral Law and the education of Jews over the centuries; it is the entry point for all subsequent legal, ethical, and theological Jewish scholarship.

The students of Rabbi Shimon bar Yocha'i asked him, "For what reason were the Jewish people in that generation deserving of annihilation?"

Rabbi Shimon said to them, "You tell me."

They said to him, "It is because they enjoyed the feast of that wicked one [Achashverosh]."

He responded, "This might be true for those in Shushan, but for those in the rest of the world, who did not participate in the feast: Why should they be killed?"

They said to him, "Then you tell us."

He said to them, "It is because they prostrated before the idol."

TEXT 3

RABBI YOSEF YITZCHAK SCHNEERSOHN, SEFER HAMAAMARIM,
YIDDISH 5701–05, VAKIBEL HAYEHUDIM, P. 149

וועגען דער סיבה וואס האט געבראכט צו אזא שלעכטען
רוחניות'דיגען מצב, זיינען פאראן צוויי דיעות: איין דיעה איז, רבי
שמעון בן יוחאי זאגט, אז דער יסוד פון דעם אידישען רוחניות'דיגען
שלעכטען צושטאנד אין יענער צייט – איז געווען וואס ביי א טייל
אידען אין די צייטן פון נבוכדנצר'ס מלוכה, איז געווען די מיינונג אז
דער עיקר קיום פון דעם מענטשען איז קראפט. דאס מיינט – אז דער
עיקר איז דער חומריות-וועלטליכער לעבן, און דער מענטש באדארף
דאס ערווארבען דורך קראפט, וואס דאס איז געווען די גרונד-מיינונג
פון נבוכדנצר'ן.

און דאס איז וואס רבי שמעון בן יוחאי זאגט, אז דער חטא פון די
אידען איז געווען וואס זיי האבען זיך געבוקט צו נבוכדנצר'ס צלם.
השתחוואה מיינט, אז מען גיט אוועק די אייגענע מיינונג צו יענעמ'ס
מיינונג, און אט די שלעכטע גרונד מיינונג האט געבראכט די אידען,
במשך הזמן, צו חילול שבת און חילול התורה והמצוות.

Rabbi Yosef Yitzchak Schneersohn (Rayatz, Frierdiker Rebbe, Previous Rebbe) 1880–1950

Chasidic rebbe, prolific writer, and Jewish activist. Rabbi Yosef Yitzchak, the 6th leader of the Chabad movement, actively promoted Jewish religious practice in Soviet Russia and was arrested for these activities. After his release from prison and exile, he settled in Warsaw, Poland, from where he fled Nazi occupation and arrived in New York in 1940. Settling in Brooklyn, Rabbi Schneersohn worked to revitalize American Jewish life. His son-in-law, Rabbi Menachem Mendel Schneerson, succeeded him as the leader of the Chabad movement.

Of the two reasons mentioned in the Talmud, Rabbi Shimon Bar Yocha'i maintains that the extreme spiritual downfall experienced by the Jews before Purim came as a result of "idolatry."

At the time, the growing opinion among Jews was that human survival came from achieving physical power and standing. In other words, they believed living a materialistic and "worldly" lifestyle was paramount. Accordingly, they felt the need to focus on their status as a means of advancing their physical lives.

The above was the foundation of Nebuchadnezzar's philosophy. And this was the Jews' sin of "bowing to [Nebuchadnezzar's] idol." Bowing means surrendering your own beliefs while allowing another's to supersede your own. Adopting such ill-grounded logic eventually led many Jews to steadily abandon their faith, carelessly desecrating their Jewish heritage and practices as they did.

A Provocative Act

TEXT 4

ESTHER 3:2, 5, 6

וְכָל עַבְדֵי הַמֶּלֶךְ אֲשֶׁר בְּשַׁעַר הַמֶּלֶךְ כֹּרְעִים וּמִשְׁתַּחֲוִים לְהָמָן, כִּי כֵן צִוָּה לוֹ הַמֶּלֶךְ. וּמָרְדֳּכַי לֹא יִכְרַע וְלֹא יִשְׁתַּחֲוֶה:

וַיַּרְא הָמָן כִּי אֵין מָרְדֳּכַי כֹּרֵעַ וּמִשְׁתַּחֲוֶה לוֹ, וַיִּמָּלֵא הָמָן חֵמָה:

וַיִּבֶז בְּעֵינָיו לִשְׁלֹחַ יָד בְּמָרְדֳּכַי לְבַדּוֹ, כִּי הִגִּידוּ לוֹ אֶת עַם מָרְדֳּכָי. וַיְבַקֵּשׁ הָמָן לְהַשְׁמִיד אֶת כָּל הַיְּהוּדִים אֲשֶׁר בְּכָל מַלְכוּת אֲחַשְׁוֵרוֹשׁ, עַם מָרְדֳּכָי:

And all the king's servants who were in the king's gate would kneel and prostrate themselves before Haman, for so had the king commanded, but Mordecai would neither kneel nor prostrate himself.

And when Haman saw that Mordecai would neither kneel nor prostrate himself before him, Haman became full of wrath.

But it seemed contemptible to him to lay hands on Mordecai alone, for they had told him Mordecai's nationality, and Haman sought to destroy all the Jews who were throughout Achashverosh's entire kingdom, Mordecai's people.

TEXT 5

TALMUD TRACTATE MEGILLAH, 12B–13A

"אִישׁ יְהוּדִי הָיָה בְּשׁוּשַׁן הַבִּירָה, וּשְׁמוֹ מָרְדֳּכַי בֶּן יָאִיר בֶּן שִׁמְעִי בֶּן קִישׁ,
אִישׁ יְמִינִי"... קָרֵי לֵיהּ יְהוּדִי – אַלְמָא מִיהוּדָה קָאָתֵי, וְקָרֵי לֵיהּ יְמִינִי
– אַלְמָא מִבִּנְיָמִין קָאָתֵי? ...

רָבָא אֲמַר: כְּנֶסֶת יִשְׂרָאֵל אָמְרָה לְאִידַּךְ גִּיסָא: רְאוּ מַה עָשָׂה לִי יְהוּדִי,
וּמַה שִּׁלֵּם לִי יְמִינִי. מַה עָשָׂה לִי יְהוּדִי – דְּלָא קַטְלֵיהּ דָּוִד לְשִׁמְעִי,
דְּאִתְיְלִיד מִינֵּיהּ מָרְדֳּכַי דְּמִיקַּנֵּי בֵּיהּ הָמָן. וּמַה שִּׁלֵּם לִי יְמִינִי – דְּלָא
קַטְלֵיהּ שָׁאוּל לַאֲגַג, דְּאִתְיְלִיד מִינֵּיהּ הָמָן דִּמְצַעֵר לְיִשְׂרָאֵל".

[Scripture states, "There was a certain Jew ("Yehudi") in the capital city Shushan whose name was Mordecai, the son of Yair, the son of Shimei, the son of Kish, a Benyaminite."]

Rava expounded, "The Congregation of Israel said, 'Look what a Yehudean has done to me and how a Benyaminite has repaid me.' 'What a Yehudean has done to me' refers to David's culpability for not killing Mordecai's grandfather, Shimei (although he was liable to the death penalty), which allowed for Mordecai's birth and his eventual incitement of Haman's jealous vendetta against the Jewish people. 'And how a Benyaminite has repaid me' refers to Saul's culpability for not immediately killing Haman's grandfather, the Amalekite king Agag."

II. THE PSYCHOLOGY OF MORDECAI AND ESTHER

Leading by Example

TEXT **6**

RABBI SHLOMO HALEVI ALKABETZ, MENOS HALEVI, PREFACE 12

> וחטא הסעודה נתקן על ידי אסתר, כדברי רב במגילה: "וישנה את
> נערותיה לטוב" – שהאכילה מאכל יהודי. כי שמה על לבה, ואסרה
> אסרה על נפשה, לבל תתגאל בפת בג המלך ובביין משתיו. ואין
> ספק כי היה זה ביזיון גדול למלך שתגעל נפשה במאכל המלך. והמן
> אפטרופוריא של תלונה זו, כמו שבא במדרש רבתי דאחשורוש אצל
> "ודתיהם שונות מכל עם". ובאמת כדאי הוא הביזיון הזה לקצף גדול,
> והיא הערה למות נפשה. ופקח עיניך, כי לא שמה נפשה בכפה על
> הבעילה כמו על האכילה, ואם שתיהן באונס. אלא שעניין האכילה –
> חטאת הקהל הוא בסעודת אחשורוש, ולכן השליכה נפשה מנגד, ולא
> נתפייסה באומרה "אנוסה אני", ועמוד על זה.

**Rabbi Shlomo Alkabetz
ca 1500–1580**

Born in Salonica, Greece. Kabbalist and poet; best known for his composition of the Shabbat hymn, *Lechah Dodi*. He eventually moved to Safed, Israel, where he was accepted into the circle of Rabbi Moshe Alshich, Rabbi Yosef Caro, and Rabbi Moshe Cordovero.

Esther's actions rectified this sin of "enjoying the feast." . . . Esther smuggled kosher food into the palace. Esther made a firm commitment to herself that she would not touch the food provided by the king.

Her behavior would have undoubtedly brought great shame to the king. Indeed, Haman seized on this when he made his pitch for the Jews to be killed, arguing that they were a fifth column. The truth is that this decision put Esther in grave danger and risked her life.

Pay attention: Esther did not display the same self-sacrifice to avoid being married to the king as she did with her insistence on eating kosher food. Due to the risk of her life, both would have been permissible, yet she chose to specifically risk her life to eat like a Jew so as to atone for the Jews' failure in this regard. She could have mollified herself that she had no choice, but she didn't.

TEXT 7

TALMUD TRACTATE SHABBAT, 88A

> "וַיִּתְיַצְּבוּ בְּתַחְתִּית הָהָר": אָמַר רַב אַבְדִּימִי בַּר חָמָא בַּר חָסָא: מְלַמֵּד
> שֶׁכָּפָה הַקָּדוֹשׁ בָּרוּךְ הוּא עֲלֵיהֶם אֶת הָהָר כְּגִיגִית, וְאָמַר לָהֶם: אִם אַתֶּם
> מְקַבְּלִים הַתּוֹרָה – מוּטָב, וְאִם לָאו – שָׁם תְּהֵא קְבוּרַתְכֶם. אָמַר רַב
> אַחָא בַּר יַעֲקֹב: מִכָּאן מוֹדָעָא רַבָּה לְאוֹרַיְיתָא. אָמַר רָבָא: אַף עַל פִּי כֵן,
> הֲדוּר קַבְּלוּהָ בִּימֵי אֲחַשְׁוֵרוֹשׁ, דִּכְתִיב: "קִיְּמוּ וְקִבְּלוּ הַיְּהוּדִים" – קִיְּמוּ
> מַה שֶּׁקִּיבְּלוּ כְּבָר.

[The verse states,] "And they stood at the lowermost part of the mountain."

Rabbi Avdimi bar Chama bar Chasa said, "This teaches us that the Holy One, Blessed be He, overturned the mountain above the Jews like a bowl and said to them, 'If you accept the Torah, excellent, and if not, over there will be your burial spot.'"

Rav Acha bar Yaakov said, "From here there is a substantial caveat to the obligation to fulfill the Torah."

Rava said, "Even so, they again accepted it willingly in the time of Achashverosh, as the verse states, '[The Jews] ordained and took upon them'—the Jews ordained what they had already taken upon themselves [through coercion at Mount Sinai]."

Transcending the Story

TEXT 8

THE REBBE, RABBI MENACHEM MENDEL SCHNEERSON, LIKUTEI SICHOT 16, P. 356

אין דעם זעלבן אופן ווי מרדכי און אסתר האבן זיך פאנאנדערגעטיילט
בנוגע זייערע פעולות צו מבטל זיין די גזירה, אזוי אויך איז דער חילוק
ביניהם בנוגע צו דער הדגשה אין דעם נס פורים, זיין אויפטו:

בא מרדכי איז די הדגשה בנס פורים דער רוחניות'דיקער "נצחון" פון
אידן – דאס וואס זיי האבן תשובה געטאן און אין אזא אופן, ביז אז
דאס האט אויפגעטאן דעם "קיימו מה שקבלו כבר", דער "הדר קבלוה
בימי אחשורוש" האט אראפגענומען די "מודעא רבה לאורייתא" פון
מתן תורה [און דערפאר האט מרדכי געוואלט אז פורים זאל זיין אסור
במלאכה – ועל דרך יום הכפורים, יום התשובה ודנתינת לוחות שניות
– עס זאל זיין א טאג אויך צו אפגעבן זיך מיט ענייני הנפש].

מה שאין כן אסתר האט מדגיש געווען אין דעם נס די הצלה פון
גזירת המן "להשמיד להרוג ולאבד את כל היהודים גו'" – די הצלת
הגופים פון אידן, ובלשון הלבוש: שהיתה הגזירה להשמיד ולהרוג את
הגופות . . . ולא את הנפשות . . . לכך כשנצלו ממנו כו'.

**Rabbi Menachem
Mendel Schneerson
1902–1994**

The towering Jewish leader of the 20th
century, known as "the Lubavitcher
Rebbe," or simply as "the Rebbe." Born
in southern Ukraine, the Rebbe escaped
Nazi-occupied Europe, arriving in the
U.S. in June 1941. The Rebbe inspired
and guided the revival of traditional
Judaism after the European devastation,
impacting virtually every Jewish
community the world over. The Rebbe
often emphasized that the performance
of just one additional good deed could
usher in the era of Mashiach. The
Rebbe's scholarly talks and writings have
been printed in more than 200 volumes.

Arguably, just as Mordecai and Esther took differing approaches in their efforts to combat the decree, they also would have emphasized different aspects of the eventual miracle.

Mordecai emphasized the unprecedented spiritual "victory" the Jews had won, namely, that their return was so complete—as the Talmud says, "They ordained what they had already taken upon themselves"—that the act of "accepting it willingly in the time of Achashverosh" managed to remove the "substantial caveat" from back at *Matan Torah*.

It was for this reason that Mordecai wanted to make the holiday of Purim a day prohibited of labor—not unlike Yom Kippur, the day of atonement and the day when, historically, the Jews received the Second Tablets [also at Mount Sinai, of course]. He intended to provide Jews, for all future generations, a day to properly dedicate their time to Purim's soul-centered nature.

Esther, however, prioritized the miracle aspect as it was expressed in the actual salvation from Haman's decree to "destroy, kill, and cause to perish all the Jews, both young and old, little children and women." In other words, Esther stressed the rescue of the Jewish *body*. As Rabbi Mordecai Yoffe writes, [contrasting the overtly spiritual Chanukah miracle of the oil], "[On Purim,] the decree was to 'destroy and kill' the Jews' bodies . . . and not their souls. . . . That's why the eventual rescue from a material threat [was commemorated with joy, expressed specifically through feasting, as opposed to Chanukah, where the eight-day miracle's spiritual nature does not require a daily meal]."

Practically in a Bind

Question for Discussion

How are we to know when to put our Judaism on the offense like Mordecai or when to be diplomatic like Esther?

III. THE MASK ON OUR EYES

Don't Be Fazed

TEXT 9

RABBI BACHYA IBN PAKUDAH, DUTIES OF THE HEART,
FOURTH TREATISE ON TRUST, INTRODUCTION

> הבוטח באלוקים, יביאנו הבטחתו עליו שלא יעבוד זולתו, ושלא יקווה
> לאיש, ולא ייחל לבני אדם, ולא יעבדם להתרצות אליהם, ולא יחניף
> להם, ולא יסכים עמהם בבלתי עבודת האלוקים, ולא יפחידהו ענيינם,
> ולא יירא ממחלוקותם. אבל יתפשט מבגדי טובותם, וטרח הודאתם,
> וחובת תגמולם, ואם יוכיח אותם – לא יזהר בכבודם, ואם יכלימם –
> לא יבוש מהם.

**Rabbi Bachya ibn Pakudah
11th century**

Moral philosopher and author. Ibn
Pakudah lived in Muslim Spain, but little
else is known about his life. *Chovot
Halevavot (Duties of the Heart)*, his major
work, was intended to be a guide for
attaining spiritual perfection. Originally
written in Judeo-Arabic and published
in 1080, it was later translated into
Hebrew and published in 1161 by Judah
ibn Tibbon, a scion of the famous family
of translators. Ibn Pakudah had a strong
influence on Jewish pietistic literature.

Absolute trust in G-d should lead you to adopt the following convictions:

To not worship anyone or thing other than G-d;

To put no hope in any person, nor depend on anyone;

To not work to win others' approval;

To not flatter them;

To not be compelled to agree when faced with something antithetical to your service of G-d;

To not be intimidated by another's social status;

To not be afraid of ideological conflict;

To free yourself from excessive expressions of gratitude and the constant need to repay others' favors;

If you need to rebuke someone, you should not be afraid of slighting them;

To not shy away even from humiliating, if necessary, so that your rebuke is effective;

And to not embellish people's false ways.

A Mordecai in Our Times

TEXT 10

RABBI YOSEF YITZCHAK SCHNEERSOHN, SEFER HASICHOT 5680, P. 4

שבאתי לחצר מות, הכניסוני לאולם גדול. כחמשה עשר אנשים
ישבו מסביב לשולחן משני עבריו – מימין ומשמאל, ובראש השולחן
ישבו שנים, ואותי הושיבו בסוף השולחן, מול השנים אשר בראשו,
ושלושת השומרים ישבו לאחוריי, מימין ומשמאל ומאמצע.

אחד מהיושבים בראש השולחן פנה אלי לאמור: אנחנו חברי "ועד
מבקרי הדתות" אשר על יד הפארטיי, ואנחנו עוסקים לבקר את דת
ישראל. היו לנו שאלות שונות, והזמנו את הרב בערמאן ואת הרב
גאלדענבערג. שאלנו מאיתם מה ששאלנו, והשיבו מה שהשיבו,
וכעת הזמנו את הרב שניאורסון, לפתור לנו איזה שאלות מדת ישראל
הקשורות עם הקבלה והחסידות. כל זה אמר בלשון רוסיא.

אנכי השבתי באידיש: כבר הודעתי – בשתי הפעמים שהייתי קרוא
אל הטשעקא מלפנים – כי לא אסור מן הפרינציפים שלי, ועוד לא
נולד ולא יוולד אותו בן אדם או שד, אשר יזיז אותי מהפרינציפים שלי
– אפילו זיז כל שהוא.

עוד טרם גמרתי את דברי, הפסיקני אחד מן המסובים אל השולחן,
שישב מימין היושב בראש השולחן, ויגביה את האקדח שהיה מונח
על השולחן מולי – כי חוץ מזה שהיו חגורים כולם בכלי זין, היה גם
אקדח מונח על השלחן לפני כל אחד מהיושבים – ויאמר: צעצוע זה
מסיר את הפרינציפים, ואימתו פותח את הפה, וגם אילם נעשה דבְּרן.

טעות גמור – השבתי – צעצוע זה עושה רושם רק על הבלתי מאמינים,
נמוגי הלב, שאין להם אלא עולם אחד והרבה אלים – אַיין וועלט און אַ
סאך געטער. כל בעל תאווה יש לו אלקיו, אבל אנחנו שיש לנו רק א-ל
אחד ומאמינים בשני עולמות, הנה צעצוע זה שאתם מראים לי – לא
לבד שאינו מבהיל, אלא גם אינו עושה רושם.

When we arrived at the courtyard of death, they led me to a
large chamber in which some fifteen people sat along both sides
of a long table. At the head of the table sat another two, and

I was seated opposite them at the foot of the table. My three guards sat behind me, left, right, and center.

One of those seated at the head of the table addressed me, "We are the members of the Party's Committee to Investigate Religions, now occupied in investigating the Jewish religion. We have various questions. We have already summoned Rabbi Berman and Rabbi Goldenberg—we asked what we asked, and they answered what they answered. Now we have summoned Rabbi Schneersohn to resolve certain issues pertaining to kabbalah and Chasidism." All this was said in the Russian language.

I answered in Yiddish, "I have already made it clear on the two former occasions on which I was summoned to the Cheka that I will not budge from my principles. There is yet to be born and never will there be born the man or demon who will move me in the slightest degree from my principles. . . ."

Before I finished my words, I was interrupted by a "committee member" seated on the right side of the table. He lifted the revolver that lay on the table—in addition to the arms that they all wore on their belts, a revolver lay on the table before each of the assembled—and pointed it at me, saying, "This toy does away with 'principles.' Fear of it has opened many a mouth. Even the dumb have become talkative before it."

"You are utterly mistaken," I replied. "This toy impresses only the cowardly atheist, who has but a single world and many gods [Yiddish: *ein velt un asach getter*]—every hedonist has his many gods. But as for us, who have but a single G-d and believe in two worlds, the toy which you are brandishing not only fails to frighten, it makes no impression whatsoever."

Ceding Ground

TEXT 11

RABBI YOEL TEITELBAUM, THE SATMAR REBBE, AL
HAGEULAH VE'AL HATEMURA, CH. 40:

אמנם הורו לנו חכמינו זכרונם לברכה כאן לימוד על לדורות, אם יתרמי
כעין זה, וכמו שקרה לנו – שידעו ידיעה ברורה שהגירוי והתחרות
באומות הוא דבר רע וסכנה גדולה, ואין דעת כנסת ישראל נוחה
הימנה, אפילו אם כרוכה הצלה בצידה. וגילו לנו חכמינו זכרונם לברכה
דעד שלא נתגלה לחכמים שבאותו הדור דמה שעשה מרדכי היה
הכרח, וכבר ניתנה למשה בסיני כל מעשה הנס ומעשה מרדכי והמן –
היה גדול התרעומות עליו על שגירה את כעסו של המן הרשע להכניס
בסכנה את כל ישראל, ואי אפשר בתשלומין וכפרה על זה . . . דאף על
פי שמרדכי היה המציל על ידי תפילות וצעקה, ועשה פעולות לבטל
הגזירה, אף על פי כן צעקו עליו צעקת מחאה ותרעומות על שגרם צער
ופחד לישראל, ואי אפשר בתשלומין.

וזה אשר לימדו לנו חכמינו זכרונם לברכה, דאפילו המצילין באמת –
לא נחשבו אחר כך למצילים, אם הם גירו חמת שונאינו והכניסו לסכנה
את הכלל כולו. דאין זה דרך הצלה על פי דרך התורה.

**Rabbi Yoel Teitelbaum
1887–1979**

Chasidic Rebbe. Rabbi Teitelbaum was
born in Sighet, Romania. Known for his
scholarship from a young age, Rabbi
Teitelbaum served as rabbi in a number
of cities before being appointed rabbi
of the city of Satmar, Romania. Rescued
from the Holocaust on the Kastner train,
Rabbi Teitelbaum settled in Williamsburg,
Brooklyn (New York), where he
reestablished the Chasidic community
of Satmar. Under his leadership, Satmar
grew from a small group to one of the
largest Chasidic communities in the
world. Rabbi Teitelbaum was known
for his strictly isolationist line and
vehement opposition to Zionism.

The Talmud records a condemnation of Mordecai to serve as
a lesson for future generations. For example, our generation
features Jews who knowingly instigate and challenge the nations—this, despite their being fully cognizant as to how dan-
gerous such behavior is.

The Talmud makes sure to tell us that such behavior is unfor-
givable, even if the rescue of the Jewish people is involved:

Until they came to know that Mordecai's actions were divinely inspired and preordained, the Jews were fully justified
in strongly resenting him for arousing the evil Haman's rage,
thereby endangering the entire Jewish nation. By revealing to
us the shouts of protests and resentment that the Jews had

toward Mordecai, the Talmud teaches us that they were right. The fear, sorrow, and trauma experienced by the Jewish people cannot be atoned for nor repaid.

The sages were teaching us that even actual rescuers are not to be recognized as such if they arouse our enemies' anger and put our community in jeopardy. We should know such rescuing is not in accordance with Torah.

A New Era

TEXT 12a

THE REBBE, RABBI MENACHEM MENDEL SCHNEERSON,
SEFER HASICHOT 5752, P. 224

> ניט קוקנדיק אויף דעם תוקף פון יהודה אין מרדכי בזמנו בזמנו, און פון
> צדיקים און אידן בכל הדורות – זיינען אין אלע דורות געוועזן הגבלות
> מן החוץ, מצד אומות העולם אין זייערע גזירות אויף אידן – רחמנא
> ליצלן, היה לא תהיה – וואס האבן ניט אלעמאל דערלאזט אידן צו זיך
> פירן מיטן גאנצן תוקף און בעה"ב'ישקייט.

Notwithstanding the firm stand taken by Judah and Mordecai in their respective times, as well as the many *tzaddikim* and Jews all throughout the ages—despite their acts of bravery, there were always outside forces that limited even these heroes. The nations we lived under were very often oppressive and at times had specific laws restricting our freedoms. This prevented Jews from fully asserting themselves and having complete agency.

TEXT 12b

THE REBBE, RABBI MENACHEM MENDEL SCHNEERSON,
SEFER HASICHOT 5752, PP. 224–225

מה שאין כן בדורנו זה ובזמננו זה, זעט מען בפועל אז עס זיינען ניטא
די בלבולים פון אמאל, און אומות העולם לאזן זיך פירן כרצונם,
און דעריבער איז עס אין הדבר תלוי אלא ברצונם פון אידן אז עס זאל זיין
"ויאחזו בה וירבו ויפרו מאד", ווי עס פירט זיך אויס בפועל בכמה וכמה
מקומות, מיטן גאנצן תוקף און ברייטקייט.

סיי במדינה זו (ארצות הברית), א מלכות של חסד, וועלכע לאזט אידן
זיך פירן ווי בא זיי קומט אויס ברצונם, ועל דרך זה בכמה וכמה מדינות
בעולם. און בשנים האחרונות זעט מען ווי אויך אין די מדינות וואו עס
זיינען פריער געוווען כמה הגבלות כו', זיינען די הגבלות אראפגעפאלן,
וכמדובר כמה פעמים.

ואדרבה: ניט נאר וואס אידן זיינען פריי צו זיך פירן ווי זיי ווילן, נאר
נאכמער – די ממשלות פון אומות העולם זיינען זיי אין דעם מסייע!

ונוסף אויף דעם וואס אידן קענען זיך פירן בדרך התורה והמצוות אין
זייערע אייגענע ד' אמות – זעט מען אויך בפועל, אז בשנים האחרונות
ווערט אלץ לייכטער און לייכטער צו אויפטאן דעם "ויאחזו בה" בכל
מקום ומקום בכל קצוי תבל, וווארום די וועלט – ניט נאר אידן, נאר אויך
אומות העולם – איז א כלי אויך אויפנעמען ענינים פון אידישקייט,
תורה ומצוות, און בנוגע צו אומות העולם – די שבע מצוות בני נח.

Today's generation has been witness to a sea change in the treatment of Jews. The obstructions to a Jew's free expression are gone, as our host nations now give us free reign to do as we please. Consequently, the onus is now on us. It is up to the Jews to "take hold of it, be fruitful, and multiply greatly" wherever they are—as is already taking place in many places with much aplomb.

The United States along with many other countries have adopted this tolerant stance. Even countries that recently restricted Jewish practices are now abolishing these laws, as we've talked about many times recently.

Not only are Jews free to follow their own destiny; moreover, world governments are now assisting us to do so!

Besides the ability to operate freely in our own spaces—it is now becoming progressively easier to "take hold" of spaces all across the globe. Across the world, people have become increasingly receptive to Judaism, Torah, and *mitzvot* in the case of Jews, and the seven laws of Noah for all people.

A New Reality Is upon Us; All You Have To Do Is Open Up Your Eyes

TEXT 13

THE REBBE, RABBI MENACHEM MENDEL SCHNEERSON,
SEFER HASICHOT 5752, P. 225

היינט דארף מען נאר אויפעפענען די אויגן, וועט מען זען ווי די גאנצע
וועלט מאנט אז יעדער איד זאל שוין שטיין אין דעם מעמד ומצב פון
גאולה האמיתית והשלימה.

Today, you only need to open your eyes and plainly see how the entire world demands that every Jew start standing up and live in a state of "complete and true redemption."

Flip Your Script

TEXT **14**

THE REBBE, RABBI MENACHEM MENDEL SCHNEERSON,
PURIM, 5740, AND 12 ADAR, 5742

מהמגילה אנו למדים, שלמרות שהיהודים "נהנו מסעודתו" . . . הרי
הנקודה העיקרית (של עם מרדכי) היא "לא יכרע ולא ישתחווה" –
זה מה שהחזיק את היהודים במשך אלפיים שנות הגלות, ועל ידי זה
שמרו על "דתיהם שונות מכל עם".

כאשר אומות העולם רואים שבני ישראל עומדים בתוקף בנוגע לכל
העניינים הקשורים עם קיום התורה והמצוות, באופן של "לא יכרע ולא
ישתחווה" – הרי זה פועל עליהם שיתנו כבוד ויקר לבני ישראל.

Notwithstanding the Jews' sin of "enjoying the feast," the *Megillah* teaches that at their core, the Jewish nation is one that "neither kneels nor prostrates." This quality of holding true to their beliefs is what enabled the Jewish people to survive 2000 years of exile and hold fast to their "heritage that is so different from any other people."

When a Jew accesses their inner "neither kneel nor prostrate oneself," the world takes notice. Standing firmly and assertively for what we believe in will engender the world's honor and respect.

9.

Ki Tisa

Today or Tomorrow?

*A Rip-Roaring Ride across the Talmudic
Sea to the Raging Waters of Life*

*Dedicated to our dear friend and partner, Reb Shaya Boymelgreen on the
occasion of his birthday on 21 Adar.*

*May he go from strength to strength and enjoy good health, happiness, nachas
from his loved ones, and success in all of his endeavors.*

PARSHA OVERVIEW

Ki Tisa

The people of Israel are told to each contribute exactly half a shekel of silver to the Sanctuary. Instructions are also given regarding the making of the Sanctuary's water basin, anointing oil, and incense. "Wisehearted" artisans Betzalel and Ahaliav are placed in charge of the Sanctuary's construction, and the people are once again commanded to keep the Shabbat.

When Moses does not return when expected from Mount Sinai, the people make a golden calf and worship it. G-d proposes to destroy the errant nation, but Moses intercedes on their behalf. Moses descends from the mountain carrying the tablets of the testimony engraved with the Ten Commandments; seeing the people dancing about their idol, he breaks the tablets, destroys the golden calf, and has the primary culprits put to death. He then returns to G-d to say: "If You do not forgive them, blot me out from the book that You have written."

G-d forgives but says that the effects of their sin will be felt for many generations. At first, G-d proposes to send His angel along with them. But Moses insists that G-d Himself accompany His people to the Promised Land.

Moses prepares a new set of tablets and once more ascends the mountain, where G-d reinscribes the covenant on these second tablets. On the mountain, Moses is also granted a vision of the divine thirteen attributes of mercy. So radiant is Moses's face, upon his return, that he must cover it with a veil, which he removes only to speak with G-d and to teach His laws to the people.

I. PRESENT REALITY OR FUTURE CONSIDERATIONS?

Fast Today, Can't Tomorrow

TEXT 1

RABBI CHAIM CHIZKIYAHU MEDINI, SEDEI CHEMED, ASIFAT
DIDIM 8:358, MAARECHET YOM HAKIPURIM 1:10

> מי שברור לו שאם יתענה צום גדליה – יזיק לו צום יום כיפור, ויהיה לו
> מחלה שנוגע לספק פיקוח נפש, ויצטרך לאכול ביום כיפור. ותענית צום
> גדליה – ברור לו שלא יזיק ולא יגרע שום דבר מהתענית. נשאל הרב
> הגאון מוהרמ"ק, דיין ומורה צדק במעזריטש, בספר אהל משה סימן
> מ"ז, אם יצום צום גדליה, ולא יחוש למה שיגרום לו שלא להתענות
> ביום הכיפורים – לפי שאם לא יתענה ביום כפור הרי הוא אנוס, או
> נימא, לא יתענה בצום גדליה כדי שיוכל להתענות ביום כיפור?

Rabbi Chaim Chizkiyahu Medini
1833–1905

Scholar and prolific author. A Jerusalem native, Rabbi Medini was born into a distinguished Sefardic family. He served as the rabbi of Constantinople and later in the Crimea, during which time he authored many volumes of Torah scholarship. His most famous work is the 18-volume *Sedei Chemed*, a comprehensive encyclopedia of the Talmud. He eventually returned to Israel where he passed away in 1905.

If one is certain that should he fast on Tzom Gedalyah, it would cause him harm on Yom Kippur, possibly driving him into a life-and-death situation and forcing him to eat on Yom Kippur—whereas he is certain that he would be able to fast on Tzom Gedalyah with no harm done—what should he do?

This question was posed to the rabbi of Mezeritch, in a responsum printed in the book *Ohel Moshe*. The parameters of the question were like this: If he does not concern himself with the consequences of fasting today, when Yom Kippur arrives perhaps he can be considered an *anus* [one who is "forced" into noncompliance, who is automatically not obligated nor culpable]. Or perhaps it's better to forgo the current, lighter fast so that he would be able to fast on Yom Kippur?

Get-out-of-Jail-Free Pass

TEXT **2**

RABBI DAVID IBN ZIMRA, RESPONSA OF THE RADBAZ, VOL. 4, §1087

> שאלה: ראובן היה חבוש בבית האסורים, ולא היה יכול לצאת להתפלל
> בעשרה ולעשות המצוות. והתחנן לפני השר או ההגמון – ולא אבה
> שמוע להניחו, זולתי יום אחד בשנה, איזה יום שיחפוץ. יורה המורה,
> איזה יום מכל ימות השנה יבחר ראובן הנזכר ללכת לבית הכנסת?

Rabbi David ibn Zimra (Radbaz)
1479–1573

Noted halachist. Radvaz was born in Spain and immigrated to Safed, Israel, upon the expulsion of the Jews from Spain in 1492. In 1513, he moved to Egypt and served as rabbi, judge, and head of the yeshiva in Cairo. He also ran many successful business ventures and was independently wealthy. In 1553, he returned to Safed where he would later be buried. He authored what would later become a classic commentary to Maimonides's code of law and wrote many halachic responsa, of which more than 10,000 are extant.

A certain Reuven was in jail and unable to pray with a *minyan* and perform other *mitzvot*. He pleaded with the minister or governor to let him free, but he was only granted a one-day pass for any day of his choice. Which day out of all the days of the year should Reuven choose to go to *shul*?

Soaking the Oil

TEXT 3a

SHEMOT (EXODUS) 30:22–25

וַיְדַבֵּר ה׳ אֶל מֹשֶׁה לֵּאמֹר:

וְאַתָּה קַח לְךָ בְּשָׂמִים רֹאשׁ, מָר דְּרוֹר חֲמֵשׁ מֵאוֹת, וְקִנְּמָן בֶּשֶׂם מַחֲצִיתוֹ חֲמִשִּׁים וּמָאתָיִם, וּקְנֵה בֶשֶׂם חֲמִשִּׁים וּמָאתָיִם:

וְקִדָּה חֲמֵשׁ מֵאוֹת בְּשֶׁקֶל הַקֹּדֶשׁ, וְשֶׁמֶן זַיִת הִין:

וְעָשִׂיתָ אֹתוֹ שֶׁמֶן מִשְׁחַת קֹדֶשׁ, רֹקַח מִרְקַחַת מַעֲשֵׂה רֹקֵחַ, שֶׁמֶן מִשְׁחַת קֹדֶשׁ יִהְיֶה:

G-d spoke to Moses, saying:

"And you, take for yourself spices of the finest sort: of pure myrrh five hundred [shekel weights]; of fragrant cinnamon half of it: two hundred and fifty [shekel weights]; of fragrant cane two hundred and fifty [shekel weights],

"And of cassia five hundred [shekel weights] according to the holy shekel, and one *hin* of olive oil.

"You shall make this into an oil of holy anointment, a perfumed compound according to the art of a perfumer; it shall be an oil of holy anointment."

TEXT 3b

RASHI, AD LOC. 30:24

> וְנֶחְלְקוּ בוֹ חַכְמֵי יִשְׂרָאֵל – רַבִּי מֵאִיר אוֹמֵר: בּוֹ שָׁלְקוּ אֶת הָעִקָּרִין.
>
> אָמַר לוֹ רַבִּי יְהוּדָה: וַהֲלֹא לָסוּךְ אֶת הָעִקָּרִין אֵינוֹ סִפֵּק?
>
> אֶלָּא שֶׁרָאוּם בְּמַיִם שֶׁלֹּא יִבְלְעוּ אֶת הַשֶּׁמֶן, וְאַחַר כָּךְ הֵצִיף עֲלֵיהֶם הַשֶּׁמֶן עַד שֶׁקָּלַט הָרֵיחַ, וְקִפְּחוֹ לַשֶּׁמֶן מֵעַל הָעִקָּרִין.

Rabbi Shlomo Yitzchaki (Rashi)
1040–1105

Most noted biblical and Talmudic commentator. Born in Troyes, France, Rashi studied in the famed *yeshivot* of Mainz and Worms. His commentaries on the Pentateuch and the Talmud, which focus on the straightforward meaning of the text, appear in virtually every edition of the Talmud and Bible.

The sages in Israel are of different opinions as to the purpose of the oil. Rabbi Meir said, "The roots were boiled in it."

Rabbi Yehudah said to him, "Surely the quantity of oil was not sufficient even to smear the roots with it.

"Rather, the roots were steeped in water so that they should not thereafter absorb the oil. The oil was then poured upon them and they were left thus until the oil absorbed their scent. They then skimmed the oil off the roots."

TEXT 4

THE REBBE, RABBI MENACHEM MENDEL SCHNEERSON, LIKUTEI SICHOT 16, P. 398

רבי מאיר זאגט, אז ווען אידן האבן געדארפט מאכן דעם שמן, האבן
זיי זיך גערעכנט בעיקר מיט'ן שלימות ווי דאס איז בהווה ביים
עשיית השמן – אז עס דארף זיין "ועשית אותו" און "מרקחת גו'",
און דערפאר איז "בו שלקו את העקרין כו'"; כאטש ס'וועט דורך דעם
פעלן אין דער שפעטערדיקער תוצאה פון "שמן משחת קודש יהיה",
ווייל עס וועט זיך ניט אנזען קיין שמן באזונדער.

דאקעגן רבי יהודה נעמט אן, אז עס דארף זיין בהווה די הכנה צום
שלימות בעתיד – און דערפאר קען מען ניט זאגן אז "בו שלקו את
העקרין", ווייל דעמאלט וועט דאך שפעטער פעלן אין דער שלימות
פון "שמן משחת קודש יהיה";

דערפאר זאגט רבי יהודה אז "שראום במים כו'", וואס הגם אז דער
"ועשית אותו" און די "מרקחת" (דער הווה) איז דאן ניט בשלימות,
דערפאר איז אבער נאכדעם דער שמן (בעתיד) בשלימות.

**Rabbi Menachem
Mendel Schneerson
1902–1994**

The towering Jewish leader of the 20th
century, known as "the Lubavitcher
Rebbe," or simply as "the Rebbe." Born
in southern Ukraine, the Rebbe escaped
Nazi-occupied Europe, arriving in the
U.S. in June 1941. The Rebbe inspired
and guided the revival of traditional
Judaism after the European devastation,
impacting virtually every Jewish
community the world over. The Rebbe
often emphasized that the performance
of just one additional good deed could
usher in the era of Mashiach. The
Rebbe's scholarly talks and writings have
been printed in more than 200 volumes.

Rabbi Meir's opinion is this: When the Jews needed to make
the oil, they were primarily concerned that the oil be perfect in
the present, and, as such, they boiled the herbs in the oil. They
weren't bothered that it would slightly diminish future results,
as the oil wouldn't later be so discernable from the herbs.

By contrast, Rabbi Yehudah holds that no matter, we must be
concerned about the future consequences. And so they couldn't
boil the herbs in the oil because it would diminish the perfection later on. As such, Rabbi Yehudah states that they first
soaked it in water; even though it would possibly detract from
the perfection at the moment, it would lend to later perfection.

II. TWO EXAMPLES

The Renter as a Custodian

TEXT 5

RASHI, SHEMOT 22:14

ולא פירש מה דינו – אם כשומר חינם, או כשומר שכר. לפיכך נחלקו
בו חכמי ישראל, שוכר כיצד משלם? רבי מאיר אומר: כשומר חינם,
ורבי יהודה אומר: כשומר שכר.

[The Torah] did not specify what the status of the renter is, whether he is judged like an unpaid custodian or like a paid custodian. So, the sages of Israel differed concerning him: How does a hirer pay [in the case of an accident]? Rabbi Meir says, "Like an unpaid custodian." Rabbi Yehudah says, "Like a paid custodian."

TEXT 6

THE REBBE, RABBI MENACHEM MENDEL SCHNEERSON,
LIKUTEI SICHOT 16, PP. 399–400

און דעריבער, לשיטת רבי מאיר אז "הווה" איז מכריע לגבי "עתיד" –
דארף אויסקומען אז די שמירה אויף וועלכער דער משכיר האט זיך
פארלאזן איז די שמירה רגילה פון א שומר חנם.

מה שאין כן לשיטת רבי יהודה, אז דער "עתיד" איז מכריע לגבי
"הווה", איז כל זמן דער משכיר איז ניט פארזיכערט אז דער חפץ וועט
זיין אפגעהיט בשמירה מעולה באופן אז אויך אז לעתיד זאל דער חפץ
זיין גאנץ – וועט ער ניט מוותר זיין אויף דעם אפילו צוליב די געלט
וואס ער באקומט בהווה.

און וויבאלד אז דער שוכר איז ניט קיין שומר חנם וואס טוט א טובת
חנם דעם מפקיד, נאר ער דינגט דעם חפץ און איז זיך משתמש מיט
אים, נעמט מען אן אז דער משכיר האט זיך פארלאזן אז ער זאל היטן
דעם חפץ מיט א שמירה מעולה.

Rabbi Meir values the present over the future [and at present, the owner is getting money and unpredictable mishaps are distant worries of the future]. As such, we assume that the type of custody the owner was relying on from the lessee [when he took the money] was that of the unpaid custodian.

Rabbi Yehudah values the future over the present. As such, so long as the owner is not confident that the object will be fully guarded from a future mishap, he would not rent out his item even for the money he's receiving right now.

Inasmuch as the lessee is not doing a favor to the owner—rather he is paying money to use the item—we assume that the owner is relying on the lessee to keep the item safe with an added level of care [akin to the paid custodian].

Zimun

TEXT 7

RABBI SHNEUR ZALMAN OF LIADI, SHULCHAN ARUCH HARAV, ORACH CHAYIM 192:1

אם . . . הם משלשה ולמעלה, שיש שבח וקילוס יותר כשמצטרפין
לברכה אחת, לפי שהם ראוים לזמן. כלומר, להזדמן יחד לצירוף ברכה
בלשון רבים.

If three or more people eat together, it is a greater praise to G-d
if they unite and give thanks to G-d together. Three people or
more is a sufficiently large group to be available to band together
and say grace.

Rabbi Shneur Zalman of Liadi (Alter Rebbe)
1745–1812

Chasidic rebbe, halachic authority, and founder of the Chabad movement. The Alter Rebbe was born in Liozna, Belarus, and was among the principal students of the Magid of Mezeritch. His numerous works include the *Tanya,* an early classic containing the fundamentals of Chabad Chasidism; and *Shulchan Aruch HaRav,* an expanded and reworked code of Jewish law.

TEXT 8

TALMUD TRACTATE BERACHOT, 45A

עד כמה מזמנין? עד כזית, ורבי יהודה אומר: עד כביצה.

How much must one eat to be considered part of the *zimun*?

Rabbi Meir said: a *kezayit* [the size of an olive].

Rabbi Yehudah said: a *kebeitsah* [the size of an egg].

Babylonian Talmud

A literary work of monumental proportions that draws upon the legal, spiritual, intellectual, ethical, and historical traditions of Judaism. The 37 tractates of the Babylonian Talmud contain the teachings of the Jewish sages from the period after the destruction of the 2nd Temple through the 5th century CE. It has served as the primary vehicle for the transmission of the Oral Law and the education of Jews over the centuries; it is the entry point for all subsequent legal, ethical, and theological Jewish scholarship.

TEXT 9

THE REBBE, RABBI MENACHEM MENDEL SCHNEERSON, LIKUTEI SICHOT 16, P. 400

לויט רבי מאיר, אז מ'רעכנט זיך מיט דעם "הווה", דארף אויסקומען
אז (מדרבנן) בשעת ס'איז דא אן ענין פון אכילה דארף מען שוין בהווה
מחוייב ווערן בזימון, און וויבאלד אז שיעור אכילה בכזית . . . גלייך
בהווה בשעת האכילה, וואס "אכילה בכזית" און מ'איז מחוייב בזימון.

דאקעגן לויט רבי יהודה, אז מען דארף נעמען אין באטראכט דעם
עתיד, איז ניט מכריע דער ענין האכילה בהווה – נאר די פעולת
ותוצאות האכילה, וואס דער תכלית האכילה איז דאך צו ווערן זאט,
או דאס בריינגט דעם חיוב "וברכת" – עס דארף זיין "אכילה שיש בה
שביעה, ואיזו זו כביצה".

Rabbi Meir values the present. Accordingly, the moment a certain sense of "eating" has been achieved, the person is already considered part of the *zimun*. Inasmuch as the usual legal amount for eating is a *kezayit* . . . as soon as that benchmark of eating has passed, the obligation of *zimun* applies.

By contrast, Rabbi Yehudah takes the future into consideration. As such, the immediate sense of eating is not the linchpin; rather, it is the *result* of eating—namely, that a person should be full. *That* is what brings about the obligation to say grace. Accordingly, we must hit the mark of "eating to be full, which is the amount of a *kebeitsah*."

III. YOU'RE BETTER THAN YOU THINK

Specifying the Sin during Confession

TEXT 10

MAIMONIDES, MISHNEH TORAH, INTRODUCTION TO THE LAWS OF TESHUVAH

> מצוה עשה אחת, והוא שישוב החוטא לפני ה' ויתודה.

It is a positive commandment that a sinner repent from their sin before G-d and confess.

TEXT 11

TALMUD TRACTATE YOMA, 86B

> וצריך לפרוט את החטא, שנאמר: "אנא, חטא העם הזה חטאה גדולה,
>
> ויעשו להם אלהי זהב" – דברי רבי יהודה בן בבא.
>
> רבי עקיבא אומר: "אשרי נשוי פשע כסוי חטאה".

During confession, one must detail the sin, as it is stated, "And Moses returned to G-d and said, 'Please, these people have sinned a great sin and have made themselves a god of gold.'" This is the statement of Rabbi Yehudah ben Bava.

Rabbi Akiva says that the verse states, "Fortunate is one whose transgression is forgiven, whose sin is hidden," [which teaches that one need not detail his sins].

Rabbi Moshe ben Maimon (Maimonides, Rambam) 1135–1204

Halachist, philosopher, author, and physician. Maimonides was born in Córdoba, Spain. After the conquest of Córdoba by the Almohads, he fled Spain and eventually settled in Cairo, Egypt. There, he became the leader of the Jewish community and served as court physician to the vizier of Egypt. He is most noted for authoring the *Mishneh Torah*, an encyclopedic arrangement of Jewish law; and for his philosophical work, *Guide for the Perplexed*. His rulings on Jewish law are integral to the formation of halachic consensus.

TEXT **12**

TOSAFOT, GITIN 35B, S.V. LEICHUSH

> ... וכן מפרט מעשיו כדי שיתבייש מחטאיו. ומאן דאמר מפני החשד
> ולכך נמי לא יפרט מעשיו, שלא יחשדוהו בשאר עבירות.

Tosafot

A collection of French and German Talmudic commentaries written during the 12th and 13th centuries. Among the most famous authors of *Tosafot* are Rabbi Yaakov Tam, Rabbi Shimshon ben Avraham of Sens, and Rabbi Yitzchak ("the Ri"). Printed in almost all editions of the Talmud, these commentaries are fundamental to basic Talmudic study.

One should specify their sins so as to be truly shamed by them. Some oppose and say not to specify so others shouldn't suspect this sinner of other sins [and thus this sinner loses credibility in other legal contexts].

Present vs. Future, Again

TEXT **13**

THE REBBE, RABBI MENACHEM MENDEL SCHNEERSON, LIKUTEI SICHOT 24, P. 241

> דער מאן דאמר אז "צריך לפרוט את מעשיו" האלט, אז וויבאלד דער
> פירוט החטא איז נוגע צו דער תשובה גופא (בהווה), אז זי זאל זיין
> טיפער און אמת'ער – רעכנט מען זיך ניט מיטן חשש שבעתיד;
>
> מה שאין כן שיטת רבי עקיבא איז ... אז מען דארף זיך רעכענען מיטן
> עתיד (ער האט אין יעדן ענין געזען גלייך (בהווה) די תוצאות שבעתיד)
> – און דעריבער, אף על פי אז מצד דעם מצב בהווה וואלט דער פירוט
> החטא געבראכט צו א טיפערער תשובה, דארף מען חושש זיין אויף
> דעם הפסד וואס וועט דערפון ארויסקומען בעתיד.

The opinion that calls for a person to specify their sin considers the added intensity that it will lend to the *teshuvah* and is not concerned with the future consequences.

By contrast, Rabbi Akiva is of the opinion that we must take the future into consideration. In every situation, he would immediately see to the future consequence. Thus, even though specifying the sin now could intensify the *teshuvah*, we must consider the future negative consequences.

Looking to the Potential, Now

TEXT 14

TALMUD TRACTATE MAKOT, 24B

שוב פעם אחת היו עולין לירושלים. כיון שהגיעו להר הצופים, קרעו בגדיהם. כיון שהגיעו להר הבית, ראו שועל שיצא מבית קדשי הקדשים. התחילו הן בוכין ורבי עקיבא מצחק. אמרו לו: מפני מה אתה מצחק? אמר להם: מפני מה אתם בוכים?

אמרו לו: מקום שכתוב בו "והזר הקרב יומת", ועכשיו שועלים הלכו בו, ולא נבכה?!

אמר להן: לכך אני מצחק. דכתיב: "ואעידה לי עדים נאמנים, את אוריה הכהן ואת זכריה בן יברכיהו". וכי מה ענין אוריה אצל זכריה, אוריה במקדש ראשון, וזכריה במקדש שני? אלא, תלה הכתוב נבואתו של זכריה בנבואתו של אוריה. באוריה כתיב: "לכן בגללכם ציון שדה תחרש וגו'". בזכריה כתיב: "עוד ישבו זקנים וזקנות ברחובות ירושלים". עד שלא נתקיימה נבואתו של אוריה, הייתי מתיירא שלא תתקיים נבואתו של זכריה. עכשיו, שנתקיימה נבואתו של אוריה – בידוע שנבואתו של זכריה מתקיימת".

בלשון הזה אמרו לו: עקיבא ניחמתנו, עקיבא ניחמתנו.

A group of scholars traveled to Jerusalem after the destruction of the Temple. When they arrived at Mount Scopus and saw the site of the Temple, they rent their garments in mourning. When they arrived at the Temple Mount, they saw a fox emerging from the site of the Holy of Holies. They began weeping, and Rabbi Akiva was laughing.

They said to him, "For what reason are you laughing?"

Rabbi Akiva replied, "For what reason are you weeping?"

They answered back, "This is the place concerning which it is written, 'And the non-priest who approaches shall die,' and now foxes walk in it; and shall we not weep?"

Rabbi Akiva said to them, "That is why I am laughing, as it is written, 'And I will take to Me faithful witnesses to attest: Uriah the priest, and Zachariah the son of Jeberechiah.' Now, what is the connection between Uriah and Zachariah?"

Rabbi Akiva proceeded to explain, "The verse established that fulfillment of the prophecy of Zachariah is dependent on fulfillment of the prophecy of Uriah. In the prophecy of Uriah it is written, 'Therefore, for your sake Zion shall be plowed as a field, and Jerusalem shall become rubble, and the Temple Mount as the high places of a forest,' where foxes are found. In the prophecy of Zachariah it is written, 'There shall yet be elderly men and elderly women sitting in the streets of Jerusalem.' Until the prophecy of Uriah with regard to the destruction of the city was fulfilled I was afraid that the prophecy of Zachariah would not be fulfilled, as the two prophecies are linked. Now that the prophecy of Uriah was fulfilled, it is evident that the prophecy of Zachariah remains valid."

The sages said to him, "Akiva, you have comforted us; Akiva, you have comforted us."

TEXT 15

THE REBBE, RABBI MENACHEM MENDEL SCHNEERSON, LIKUTEI SICHOT 24, P. 242

און דעריבער: לשיטת רבי עקיבא, אז עתיד איז מכריע את ההווה –
רבי עקיבא "זעט" אינעם הווה זיין פנימיות, וואס וועט ארויסקומען
בעתיד – זעט ער אויך די פנימיות פון ענין התשובה, אז אף על פי אז
מ'האלט ערשט ביי דער דרגא הנמוכה פון תשובה . . . איז עס "בכח"
ובפנימיות שוין אן ענין פון תשובה מאהבה . . . און דעריבער האלט ער
אז אין צריך לפרוט את מעשיו.

Rabbi Akiva, who always takes the future into consideration, looks to the inner reality and what will come about in the future. In the context of *teshuvah*, Rabbi Akiva sees the inner truth of *teshuvah*, and so, even if the person experiences a lower level of *teshuvah*, its potential and inner truth is a much deeper type of *teshuvah* . . . and, as such, he holds that the person need not specify their sin.

10.

Vayakhel-Pekudei

The People Always Come First.
Except for When They Don't

A True Leader Isn't Concerned about Being a True Leader

Dedicated to Reb Hershel Lazaroff on the occasion of his birthday on 25 Adar.

May he go from strength to strength and enjoy good health, happiness, nachas from his loved ones, and success in all of his endeavors.

PARSHA OVERVIEW

Vayakhel - Pekudei

Moses assembles the people of Israel and reiterates to them the commandment to observe the Shabbat. He then conveys G-d's instructions regarding the making of the Mishkan (Tabernacle). The people donate the required materials in abundance, bringing gold, silver, and copper; blue-, purple-, and red-dyed wool; goat hair, spun linen, animal skins, wood, olive oil, herbs, and precious stones. Moses has to tell them to stop giving.

A team of wise-hearted artisans make the Mishkan and its furnishings (as detailed in the previous Torah readings of Terumah, Tetzaveh, and Ki Tisa): three layers of roof coverings; forty-eight gold-plated wall panels, and a hundred silver foundation sockets; the *parochet* (veil) that separates between the Sanctuary's two chambers, and the *masach* (screen) that is before it; the ark and its cover with the Cherubim; the table and its showbread; the seven-branched menorah with its specially prepared oil; the golden altar and the incense burned on it; the anointing oil; the outdoor altar for burnt offerings and all its implements; the hangings, posts, and foundation sockets for the courtyard; and the basin and its pedestal, made out of copper mirrors.

An accounting is made of the gold, silver, and copper donated by the people for the making of the Mishkan. Betzalel, Ahaliav, and their assistants make the eight priestly garments—the ephod, breastplate, cloak, crown, turban, tunic, sash, and breeches—according to the specifications communicated to Moses in the *parsha* of Tetzaveh.

The Mishkan is completed, and all its components are brought to Moses, who erects it, anoints it with the holy anointing oil, and initiates Aaron and his four sons into the priesthood. A cloud appears over the Mishkan, signifying the Divine Presence that has come to dwell within it.

I. LAZY PRINCES?

When the Jews Donated Too Much

TEXT 1

SHEMOT (EXODUS) 36:4–7

וַיָּבֹאוּ כָּל הַחֲכָמִים הָעֹשִׂים אֵת כָּל מְלֶאכֶת הַקֹּדֶשׁ, אִישׁ אִישׁ מִמְּלַאכְתּוֹ
אֲשֶׁר הֵמָּה עֹשִׂים:

וַיֹּאמְרוּ אֶל מֹשֶׁה לֵּאמֹר, מַרְבִּים הָעָם לְהָבִיא, מִדֵּי הָעֲבֹדָה לַמְּלָאכָה
אֲשֶׁר צִוָּה ה' לַעֲשֹׂת אֹתָהּ:

וַיְצַו מֹשֶׁה, וַיַּעֲבִירוּ קוֹל בַּמַּחֲנֶה לֵּאמֹר, אִישׁ וְאִשָּׁה אַל יַעֲשׂוּ עוֹד מְלָאכָה
לִתְרוּמַת הַקֹּדֶשׁ, וַיִּכָּלֵא הָעָם מֵהָבִיא:

וְהַמְּלָאכָה הָיְתָה דַיָּם, לְכָל הַמְּלָאכָה לַעֲשׂוֹת אֹתָהּ, וְהוֹתֵר:

Then all the wise men who were doing the work of the Holy came, each one from his work that they had been doing.

And they spoke to Moses, saying, "The people are bringing very much, more than is enough for the labor of the articles that G-d had commanded to do."

So Moses commanded, and they announced in the camp, saying, "Let no man or woman do any more work for the offering for the Holy." So the people stopped bringing.

And the work was sufficient for them for all the work, to do it and to leave over.

The Princes' Gift

TEXT **2**

IBID., 35:23–28

וְכָל אִישׁ אֲשֶׁר נִמְצָא אִתּוֹ תְּכֵלֶת וְאַרְגָּמָן, וְתוֹלַעַת שָׁנִי וְשֵׁשׁ וְעִזִּים,
וְעֹרֹת אֵילִם מְאָדָּמִים וְעֹרֹת תְּחָשִׁים – הֵבִיאוּ:

כָּל מֵרִים תְּרוּמַת כֶּסֶף וּנְחֹשֶׁת הֵבִיאוּ אֵת תְּרוּמַת ה', וְכֹל אֲשֶׁר נִמְצָא
אִתּוֹ עֲצֵי שִׁטִּים לְכָל מְלֶאכֶת הָעֲבֹדָה הֵבִיאוּ:

וְכָל אִשָּׁה חַכְמַת לֵב בְּיָדֶיהָ טָווּ, וַיָּבִיאוּ מַטְוֶה, אֶת הַתְּכֵלֶת וְאֶת הָאַרְגָּמָן
אֶת תּוֹלַעַת הַשָּׁנִי וְאֶת הַשֵּׁשׁ:

וְכָל הַנָּשִׁים אֲשֶׁר נָשָׂא לִבָּן אֹתָנָה בְּחָכְמָה, טָווּ אֶת הָעִזִּים:

וְהַנְּשִׂאִם הֵבִיאוּ אֵת אַבְנֵי הַשֹּׁהַם וְאֵת אַבְנֵי הַמִּלֻּאִים, לָאֵפוֹד וְלַחֹשֶׁן:

וְאֶת הַבֹּשֶׂם וְאֶת הַשָּׁמֶן לְמָאוֹר, וּלְשֶׁמֶן הַמִּשְׁחָה וְלִקְטֹרֶת הַסַּמִּים:

And every man with whom was found blue, purple, or crimson wool, linen, goat hair, ram skins dyed red, or *tachash* skins brought them.

Everyone who set aside an offering of silver or copper brought the offering for G-d, and everyone with whom acacia wood was found for any work of the service brought it.

And every wise-hearted woman spun with her hands, and they brought spun material: blue, purple, and crimson wool and linen.

And all the women whose hearts uplifted them with wisdom spun the goat hair.

And the princes brought the *shoham* stones and filling stones for the ephod and for the *choshen*.

And the spice and the oil for lighting and for the anointing oil and for the incense.

"Laziness" Corrected

TEXT 3

RASHI, SHEMOT (EXODUS) 35:27

> "וְהַנְּשִׂאָם הֵבִיאוּ": אמר רבי נתן: מה ראו נשיאים להתנדב בחנוכת
> המזבח בתחלה, ובמלאכת המשכן לא התנדבו בתחלה? אלא כך
> אמרו נשיאים: יתנדבו ציבור מה שמתנדבין, ומה שמחסירים – אנו
> משלימין אותו. כיון שהשלימו ציבור את הכל, שנאמר (שמות לו ז):
> "וְהַמְּלָאכָה הָיְתָה דַיָּם", אמרו נשיאים: מה עלינו לעשות? הביאו את
> אבני השוהם וגו'. לכך התנדבו בחנוכת המזבח תחלה. ולפי שנתעצלו
> מתחילה, נחסרה אות משמם, "וְהַנְּשִׂאָם" כתיב.

Rabbi Shlomo Yitzchaki (Rashi)
1040–1105

Most noted biblical and Talmudic commentator. Born in Troyes, France, Rashi studied in the famed *yeshivot* of Mainz and Worms. His commentaries on the Pentateuch and the Talmud, which focus on the straightforward meaning of the text, appear in virtually every edition of the Talmud and Bible.

Rabbi Natan said: What prompted the princes to donate for the dedication of the altar first while they did not donate first for the work of the Mishkan?

This is what the princes said, "Let the community donate what they will donate, and whatever they are missing, we will complete." Since the community completed everything, as it is said, "And the work was sufficient," the princes said, "What are we to do?" So they brought the *shoham* stones, etc.

Therefore, they brought [donations] first for the dedication of the altar. Inasmuch as they were lazy the first time [i.e., they did not immediately donate], a letter is missing from their name, and וְהַנְּשִׂאָם is written [instead of וְהַנְּשִׂיאִם, with the additional *yud*].

The Twelve Days of Dedication

TEXT **4**

BAMIDBAR (NUMBERS) 7:10–17

וַיַּקְרִיבוּ הַנְּשִׂאִים אֵת חֲנֻכַּת הַמִּזְבֵּחַ בְּיוֹם הִמָּשַׁח אֹתוֹ, וַיַּקְרִיבוּ הַנְּשִׂיאִם אֶת קָרְבָּנָם לִפְנֵי הַמִּזְבֵּחַ:

וַיֹּאמֶר ה' אֶל מֹשֶׁה, נָשִׂיא אֶחָד לַיּוֹם, נָשִׂיא אֶחָד לַיּוֹם, יַקְרִיבוּ אֶת קָרְבָּנָם לַחֲנֻכַּת הַמִּזְבֵּחַ:

וַיְהִי הַמַּקְרִיב בַּיּוֹם הָרִאשׁוֹן אֶת קָרְבָּנוֹ, נַחְשׁוֹן בֶּן עַמִּינָדָב לְמַטֵּה יְהוּדָה:

וְקָרְבָּנוֹ, קַעֲרַת כֶּסֶף אַחַת שְׁלֹשִׁים וּמֵאָה מִשְׁקָלָהּ, מִזְרָק אֶחָד כֶּסֶף שִׁבְעִים שֶׁקֶל בְּשֶׁקֶל הַקֹּדֶשׁ, שְׁנֵיהֶם מְלֵאִים סֹלֶת בְּלוּלָה בַשֶּׁמֶן לְמִנְחָה:

כַּף אַחַת עֲשָׂרָה זָהָב, מְלֵאָה קְטֹרֶת:

פַּר אֶחָד בֶּן בָּקָר, אַיִל אֶחָד, כֶּבֶשׂ אֶחָד בֶּן שְׁנָתוֹ לְעֹלָה:

שְׂעִיר עִזִּים אֶחָד לְחַטָּאת:

וּלְזֶבַח הַשְּׁלָמִים בָּקָר שְׁנַיִם, אֵילִם חֲמִשָּׁה, עַתּוּדִים חֲמִשָּׁה, כְּבָשִׂים בְּנֵי שָׁנָה חֲמִשָּׁה, זֶה קָרְבַּן נַחְשׁוֹן בֶּן עַמִּינָדָב:

The chieftains brought [offerings for] the dedication of the altar on the day it was anointed; the chieftains presented their offerings in front of the altar.

G-d said to Moses, "One chieftain each day, one chieftain each day, shall present his offering for the dedication of the altar."

The one who brought his offering on the first day was Nahshon, the son of Amminadab of the tribe of Judah.

And his offering was one silver bowl weighing one hundred and thirty [shekels], one silver sprinkling basin [weighing] seventy shekels according to the holy shekel, both filled with fine flour mixed with olive oil for a meal offering.

One spoon [weighing] ten [shekels] of gold filled with incense.

One young bull, one ram, and one lamb in its first year for a burnt offering.

One young he-goat for a sin offering.

And for the peace offering: two oxen, five rams, five he-goats, five lambs in their first year; this was the offering of Nahshon, the son of Amminadab.

II. SELFLESS LEADERSHIP

Donating First vs. Last

Question for Discussion

What's the best way for the princes to lead the Mishkan's construction: Donating first, or waiting until the end to see what the congregation manages to accomplish and then filling in the rest?

Moses's Mission

TEXT 5a

SHEMOT (EXODUS) 19:10–14

וַיֹּאמֶר ה' אֶל מֹשֶׁה, לֵךְ אֶל הָעָם, וְקִדַּשְׁתָּם הַיּוֹם וּמָחָר, וְכִבְּסוּ שִׂמְלֹתָם:

וְהָיוּ נְכֹנִים לַיּוֹם הַשְּׁלִישִׁי, כִּי בַּיּוֹם הַשְּׁלִישִׁי יֵרֵד ה' לְעֵינֵי כָל הָעָם עַל הַר סִינָי:

וְהִגְבַּלְתָּ אֶת הָעָם סָבִיב לֵאמֹר, הִשָּׁמְרוּ לָכֶם עֲלוֹת בָּהָר וּנְגֹעַ בְּקָצֵהוּ, כָּל הַנֹּגֵעַ בָּהָר מוֹת יוּמָת:

לֹא תִגַּע בּוֹ יָד, כִּי סָקוֹל יִסָּקֵל אוֹ יָרֹה יִיָּרֶה, אִם בְּהֵמָה אִם אִישׁ לֹא יִחְיֶה, בִּמְשֹׁךְ הַיֹּבֵל, הֵמָּה יַעֲלוּ בָהָר:

וַיֵּרֶד מֹשֶׁה מִן הָהָר אֶל הָעָם, וַיְקַדֵּשׁ אֶת הָעָם וַיְכַבְּסוּ שִׂמְלֹתָם:

And G-d said to Moses, "Go to the people and prepare them today and tomorrow, and they shall wash their garments.

"And they shall be prepared for the third day, for on the third day, the L-rd will descend before the eyes of all the people upon Mount Sinai.

"And you shall set boundaries for the people around, saying, 'Beware of ascending the mountain or touching its edge; whoever touches the mountain shall surely be put to death.'

"No hand shall touch it, for he shall be stoned or cast down; whether man or beast, he shall not live. When the ram's horn sounds a long, drawn-out blast, they may ascend the mountain."

So Moses descended from the mountain to the people, and he prepared the people, and they washed their garments.

TEXT 5b

RASHI, AD LOC.

> "מן ההר אל העם": מלמד שלא היה משה פונה לעסקיו, אלא מן ההר
> אל העם.

"From the mountain to the people." This teaches us that Moses did not turn to his own affairs but went directly from the mountain to the people.

Putting aside Spiritual Needs

TEXT 6

THE REBBE, RABBI MENACHEM MENDEL SCHNEERSON, LIKUTEI SICHOT 16, P. 428

> וואס לכאורה איז ניט מובן: מאי קא משמע לן, אז משה האט גלייך
> איברגעגעבן די שליחות פון אויבערשטן צו אידן און ניט פונה געוועוען
> פריער צו זיינע אייגענע עסקים? – נאר דער ענין וחידוש איז, "לא
> היה פונה לעסקיו" [מיינט ניט (נאר) צו זיינע צרכי הגוף וכו', נאר אויך]
> צו זיינע עסקים אין דעם ענין ושליחות גופא – זיינע הכנות צו מתן
> תורה, כולל אויך (ובפרט) צו זיין ראוי צו "משה קבל תורה מסיני".

Rabbi Menachem Mendel Schneerson
1902–1994

The towering Jewish leader of the 20th century, known as "the Lubavitcher Rebbe," or simply as "the Rebbe." Born in southern Ukraine, the Rebbe escaped Nazi-occupied Europe, arriving in the U.S. in June 1941. The Rebbe inspired and guided the revival of traditional Judaism after the European devastation, impacting virtually every Jewish community the world over. The Rebbe often emphasized that the performance of just one additional good deed could usher in the era of Mashiach. The Rebbe's scholarly talks and writings have been printed in more than 200 volumes.

Seemingly, we can ask: What's so exceptional about the fact that Moses didn't take care of his own needs before carrying out a G-d–given mission to the Jewish people?

The answer is this: "Not taking care of his own needs" means [not (only) that he didn't take care of personal, material needs but] that he didn't even take care of the needs pertinent to this very mission—his spiritual preparations for receiving the Torah, including (and specifically,) rendering himself fit to "receive the Torah from [Mount] Sinai."

Focusing on the Mission

TEXT 7

THE REBBE, RABBI MENACHEM MENDEL SCHNEERSON, IBID.

> דער ערשטער תפקיד פון די נשיאים איז געווען צו זארגן . . . אז אידן
> זאלן מנדב זיין וויפיל זיי קענען . . . און דאן ערשט האבן זיי אנגעהויבן
> טראכטן וועגן זייער השתתפות בנדבת המשכן – "הביאו את אבני
> השוהם כו'".

The princes' first concern was to get . . . the community to donate as much as they could. . . . Only then did they start thinking about their own contribution for the Mishkan—at which point they brought the *shoham* stones.

A Campaign for Material, No Cash

TEXT 8

RABBI CHAYIM IBN ATAR, OR HACHAYIM, SHEMOT (EXODUS) 35:21

> יודיע הכתוב כי כל צרכי המשכן כו' באו בעצמן בנדבה, ולא הוצרכו
> לקנות מהם בכסף וזהב המובא בתרומה.

The Torah tells us that all the raw materials necessary for the Mishkan's construction were donated; none of them had to be purchased with contributed funds.

Rabbi Chayim ibn Atar (*Or Hachayim*) 1696–1743

Biblical exegete, kabbalist, and Talmudist. Rabbi Atar, born in Meknes, Morocco, was a prominent member of the Moroccan rabbinate and later immigrated to the Land of Israel. He is most famous for his *Or Hachayim*, a popular commentary on the Torah. The famed Jewish historian and bibliophile Rabbi Chaim Yosef David Azulai was among his most notable disciples.

TEXT 9a

THE REBBE, RABBI MENACHEM MENDEL SCHNEERSON, LIKUTEI SICHOT 16, P. 429

און דאס איז דער פירוש פון "השלימו ציבור את הכל, שנאמר: והמלאכה היתה דים": אויך די זאכן פון די י"ג דברים וואס ביי זיי איז ניט געווען, האבן די אידן משלים געווען דורך מנדב זיין א ריבוי כסף וכו', ביז צו געבן אויך דעם פולן פרייז פון די אבני שוהם, אבני מילואים וכו'.

When we say, "the community completed everything" and "the work was sufficient," we mean this: even for items from the thirteen special materials that they did not have on hand, the Jewish people met the need by donating lots of silver, etc., including the amount necessary to purchase the *shoham* stones and the filling stones, etc.

The Downside of the Princes' Gift

TEXT 9b

THE REBBE, RABBI MENACHEM MENDEL SCHNEERSON, IBID., P. 430

און דערפאר האבן די נשיאים געפילט אז זיי האבן ניט קיין גלייכע
השתתפות אין נדבת המשכן מיט אלע אידן: אידן האבן דאך געגעבן
דאס וואס איז געווען מוכרח פארן משכן, מה שאין כן די נדבת
הנשיאים איז שוין ניט געווען אין גדר פון הכרחיות, היות אז דער כסף
כו' אויך קויפען אבני שוהם כו', איז שוין געווען (און זייער השתתפות
איז געווען אין דעם וואס זיי האבן בפועל געבראכט די אבני שוהם וכו',
פארשפארט דעם קויפן).

The princes felt their part in donating to the Mishkan didn't
equal up to everyone else's: When everyone else donated [their
materials], they were really meeting the needs of the Mishkan.
But when the princes donated, there was no longer such a need
because there was already enough money [in the coffers] to
purchase the *shoham* stones, etc. (It emerges that their role was
simply to bring the actual stones, taking away the need to go
out and buy them.)

III. MEETING THE NEEDS OF THE PEOPLE

The Mishkan: A Symbol of Forgiveness

TEXT 10

MIDRASH TANCHUMA, TERUMAH 8

אָמַר רַבִּי יְהוּדָה בְּרַבִּי שָׁלוֹם: . . . בְּיוֹם הַכִּפּוּרִים נֶאֱמַר לְמֹשֶׁה "וְעָשׂוּ לִי
מִקְדָּשׁ". . . וְאַתָּה מוֹצֵא, שֶׁבְּיוֹם הַכִּפּוּרִים נִתְכַּפֵּר לָהֶם, וּבוֹ בַּיּוֹם אָמַר
לוֹ הַקָּדוֹשׁ בָּרוּךְ הוּא "וְעָשׂוּ לִי מִקְדָּשׁ וְשָׁכַנְתִּי בְּתוֹכָם", כְּדֵי שֶׁיֵּדְעוּ
כָּל הָאֻמּוֹת שֶׁנִּתְכַּפֵּר לָהֶם עַל מַעֲשֵׂה הָעֵגֶל. וּלְכָךְ נִקְרָא מִשְׁכַּן הָעֵדוּת,
שֶׁהוּא עֵדוּת לְכָל בָּאֵי הָעוֹלָם שֶׁהַקָּדוֹשׁ בָּרוּךְ הוּא שׁוֹכֵן בְּמִקְדָּשְׁכֶם.

Rabbi Yehudah said in the name of Rabbi Shalom: On Yom Kippur, Moses was told, "They shall make Me a sanctuary." . . . Thus, it was on Yom Kippur that the Jewish people were forgiven, and it was on that very day that G-d said, "They shall make Me a sanctuary, and I will dwell among them"—so that the nations of the world should see that He forgave the Jewish people for the golden calf.

This is why the Tabernacle is called the "Tabernacle of Testimony," because it serves as testimony to the whole world that G-d dwells in the Sanctuary of the Jewish people.

Tanchuma

A Midrashic work bearing the name of Rabbi Tanchuma, a 4th-century Talmudic sage quoted often in this work. "Midrash" is the designation of a particular genre of rabbinic literature usually forming a running commentary on specific books of the Bible. *Tanchuma* provides textual exegeses, expounds upon the biblical narrative, and develops and illustrates moral principles. *Tanchuma* is unique in that many of its sections commence with a halachic discussion, which subsequently leads into nonhalachic teachings.

An Anxious Nation

TEXT 11

RASHI, VAYIKRA (LEVITICUS) 9:23

> שכל שבעת ימי המלואים, שהעמידו משה למשכן ושימש בו ופרקו
> בכל יום, לא שרתה בו שכינה, והיו ישראל נכלמים ואומרים למשה:
> משה רבינו, כל הטורח שטרחנו שתשרה שכינה בינינו ונדע שנתכפר
> לנו עון העגל! לכך אמר להם ... אהרן אחי כדאי וחשוב ממני, שעל ידי
> קרבנותיו ועבודתו תשרה שכינה בכם, ותדעו שהמקום בחר בו.

Throughout all seven days of the investitures [preceding the inauguration], when Moses erected the Mishkan, performed the service in it, and then dismantled it daily, the *Shechinah* did not rest in it. The Israelites were humiliated, and they said to Moses, "Moses, our teacher, all the efforts we have taken were so that the *Shechinah* should dwell among us, so that we would know that we have been forgiven for the sin of the [golden] calf!"

Therefore, Moses answered them, "My brother Aaron is more worthy and important than I, insofar as through his offerings and his service, the *Shechinah* will dwell among you, and you will know that G-d has chosen him."

Urgency Is Key

TEXT 12

THE REBBE, RABBI MENACHEM MENDEL SCHNEERSON, LIKUTEI SICHOT 16, P. 430

> הן אמת אז דער תפקיד פון נשיא העדה או השבט איז צו באווארענען
> אז אידן זאלן טאן די ענינים המוטלים עליהם, האבן די נשיאים
> צוזאמען דערמיט געדארפט באווארענען אויך די זריזות אין בנין
> המשכן, אז עס זאלן גרייט זיין אלע זאכן וואס מ'דארף האבן למלאכת
> המשכן בפועל ובהקדם.
>
> און דערפאר האט דא ניט מתאים געווען דער סדר ההנהגה פון ווארטן
> כמה וכמה זמן און זען וואס "יתנדבו ציבור מה שמתנדבים, ומה
> שמחסרין אנו משלימין אותו" –
>
> מצד זייער תפקיד אלס נשיאים גופא האט זיך געפאדערט, אז
> מאנענדיק ביי אידן ("יתנדבו ציבור מה שמתנדבין") דארפן זיי
> גלייכצייטיק זיך מקדים זיין צו ברענגען זייער נדבה, כדי אז דער משכן
> זאל אויפגעבויט ווערן בהקדם הכי אפשרי.

True, a leader's job is to make sure the Jewish people fulfill their responsibilities. But at the same time, the princes should have taken care to build the Mishkan quickly, making sure everything needed was ready as soon as possible.

Therefore, in this case, waiting around for "the community [to] donate what they will donate, and whatever they are missing, we will complete" was out of place.

Precisely because they were leaders, even as they encouraged the Jewish people (to "donate as much as they could"), they ought to have simultaneously hurried to bring their own gift, so that the Mishkan could be completed as soon as possible.

Conclusion: Become an Onion If Need Be

TEXT **13**

THE REBBE, RABBI MENACHEM MENDEL SCHNEERSON,
TORAT MENACHEM 5715:1, PP. 313–314

כיון שאדמו"ר האמצעי היה מונח בהפצת תורת החסידות בכל
מקום, צוה לכל החסידים שבאו אליו, אשר, בלכתם או בנסעם בחזרה
לעיירתם, הנה בכל מקום שעוברים בדרכם יחזרו שם חסידות.

פעם אחת בא אליו אחד החסידים בשאלת הוראה כיצד עליו להתנהג
– שכן, כאשר חוזר המאמר חסידות, ורואה כיצד פועל הדבר על
השומעים, נעשה אצלו רגש של סיפוק נפשי: הוא מרגיש את
מציאותו, שפעל איזה ענין; הוא קלט את המאמר בטוב, וחזר אותו
מתוך חיות, כך שפעל גם על השומעים, ומזה נעשה אצלו הרגש של
ישות, ואפילו הרגש של גאוה.

מספרים חסידים שאדמו"ר האמצעי השיב לו: "א ציבעלע זאל פון
דיר ווערן, אבער חסידות זאלסטו חזר'ן".

The Miteler Rebbe [Rabbi Dovber of Lubavitch, second Chabad
Rebbe] embarked on a campaign to disseminate the teachings
of *Chasidut* throughout the world. To this end, he instructed
all of his Chasidim—when they would visit Lubavitch—to
teach *Chasidut* publicly in every town they would pass on the
way home.

One of the Chasidim who would recite the Chasidic teachings
noticed the positive effect his words had on his listeners, and
he approached the Rebbe with a question: He had a very good
grasp of the material, and he had a talent for teaching it to others in an impactful way. Thus, he was starting to feel proud,
even somewhat egotistic about it.

Chasidim relate that the Miteler Rebbe answered him, "Even if
you become like an onion, you should still teach *Chasidut*."

11.

Vayikra

When Humility Isn't Healthy and Pride Is Perfect

When You're Truly Small, Then You're Really Big

Dedicated to Mr. Howard Jonas in appreciation of his friendship and partnership with JLI and his dedication to bringing the light of Torah to communities across the globe.

PARSHA OVERVIEW

Vayikra

G-d calls to Moses from the Tent of Meeting and communicates to him the laws of the *korbanot*, the animal and meal offerings brought in the Sanctuary. These include:

1. The "ascending offering" (*olah*), that was wholly raised to G-d by the fire atop the altar;

2. Five varieties of "meal offering" (*minchah*), prepared with fine flour, olive oil, and frankincense;

3. The "peace offering" (*shelamim*), whose meat was eaten by the one bringing the offering, after parts were burned on the altar and parts were given to the *kohanim* (priests);

4. The different types of "sin offering" (*chatat*) brought to atone for transgressions committed erroneously by the High Priest, the entire community, the king, or the ordinary Jew;

5. The "guilt offering" (*asham*), brought by one who misappropriated property of the Sanctuary, who was in doubt as to whether he transgressed a divine prohibition, or who committed a "betrayal against G-d" by swearing falsely to defraud a fellow man.

I. A TALE OF TWO LETTERS

A Small Alef

TEXT 1

VAYIKRA (LEVITICUS) 1:1

וַיִּקְרָא אֶל מֹשֶׁה, וַיְדַבֵּר ה' אֵלָיו מֵאֹהֶל מוֹעֵד, לֵאמֹר:

And He called to Moses, and G-d spoke to him from the Tent of Meeting, saying . . .

Moses's Humility

TEXT 2

RABBI ABRAHAM SABA, TZEROR HAMOR, VAYIKRA, LOC. CIT.

ואולי הטעם שזאת האלף קטנה, הוא מה שכתבתי למעלה – שמשה בענוותנותו הרחיק עצמו מהשררה, והיה בורח ומקטין עצמו, עד שהוצרך ה' לקוראו. ולזה כתב בכאן "ויקרא אל משה" באלף קטנה.

Rabbi Abraham Saba
1440–1508

Bible commentator and preacher. Born in Castile, Spain, Rabbi Abraham Saba was a prolific writer, but his manuscripts were lost as he fled from Spain and Portugal when the Jews were expelled. Settling in Fès, Morocco, he reproduced many of his lost works, including his Torah commentary *Tzeror Hamor*.

Perhaps the reason for the small *alef* is in line with what I wrote previously, namely, that out of his great humility, Moses distanced himself from any sort of prestige. He fled from the stage so much that G-d had to call out to him. Thus, the *alef* of the word *Vayikra*—and he called—is small.

TEXT 3

SHEMOT (EXODUS) 3:9–11

> וְעַתָּה, הִנֵּה צַעֲקַת בְּנֵי יִשְׂרָאֵל בָּאָה אֵלָי, וְגַם רָאִיתִי אֶת הַלַּחַץ אֲשֶׁר
> מִצְרַיִם לֹחֲצִים אֹתָם:
>
> וְעַתָּה לְכָה וְאֶשְׁלָחֲךָ אֶל פַּרְעֹה, וְהוֹצֵא אֶת עַמִּי בְנֵי יִשְׂרָאֵל מִמִּצְרָיִם:
>
> וַיֹּאמֶר מֹשֶׁה אֶל הָאֱלֹקִים, מִי אָנֹכִי כִּי אֵלֵךְ אֶל פַּרְעֹה, וְכִי אוֹצִיא אֶת בְּנֵי
> יִשְׂרָאֵל מִמִּצְרָיִם:

"And now, behold, the cry of the Children of Israel has come to Me, and I have also seen the oppression that the Egyptians are oppressing them.

So now come, and I will send you to Pharaoh, and take My people, the Children of Israel, out of Egypt."

But Moses said to G-d, "Who am I that I should go to Pharaoh, and that I should take the Children of Israel out of Egypt?"

A Big Alef

TEXT 4

I DIVREI HAYAMIM (I CHRONICLES) 1:1

> אָדָם, שֵׁת, אֱנוֹשׁ:

Adam, Seth, Enosh.

II. THE ALTER REBBE'S ANSWER

A Teaching Moment from Grandfather

TEXT 5

THE REBBE, RABBI MENACHEM MENDEL SCHNEERSON, LIKUTEI SICHOT 17, PP. 1-2

Rabbi Menachem Mendel Schneerson 1902–1994

The towering Jewish leader of the 20th century, known as "the Lubavitcher Rebbe," or simply as "the Rebbe." Born in southern Ukraine, the Rebbe escaped Nazi-occupied Europe, arriving in the U.S. in June 1941. The Rebbe inspired and guided the revival of traditional Judaism after the European devastation, impacting virtually every Jewish community the world over. The Rebbe often emphasized that the performance of just one additional good deed could usher in the era of Mashiach. The Rebbe's scholarly talks and writings have been printed in more than 200 volumes.

דער רבי האט אמאל דערצײלט (אין א פסח'דיקן פארברענגען) דעם סדר װי דער אלטער רבי האט אריינגעפירט זיין אייניקל, כבוד קדושת אדמו"ר הצמח צדק, אין חדר. צווישן די זאכן וואס דער רבי האט דאן דערצײלט איז, אז דער אלטער רבי האט געהייסן דעם מלמד ער זאל לערנען מיטן קינד די ערשטע פרשה פון ויקרא. נאך דעם וי דער מלמד האט אפגעלערנט די פרשה מיטן קינד, האט דאס קינד געפרעגט בא דעם אלטן רבי'ן: פארוואס איז דער וַוארט "ויקרא" מיט אן אל"ף זעירא?

דער רבי האט זיך פאר'דבק'ט א היפשע צײט, און נאכדעם האט ער געזאגט:

אדם הראשון איז געווען יציר כפיו של הקדוש ברוך הוא, און הקדוש ברוך הוא איז מעיד עליו אז חכמתו מרובה מחכמת מלאכי השרת. ער – אדם הראשון – האט געוואוסט מעלת עצמו און האט זיך מיט דעם בא זיך אליין איבערגענומען, איז ער דורכגעפאלן אין חטא עץ הדעת.

משה רבינו . . . האט אויך געוואוסט מעלת עצמו, איז ניט נאר וואס משה רבינו האט זיך ניט איבערגענומען בא זיך אליין מיט דעם, אדרבה, דאס האט אים געמאכט א "לב נשבר ונדכה" וואס ער איז געווען שפל בעיני עצמו, טראכטנדיק, אז אן אנדער איד, ניט עמרם'ס א זון און ניט אברהם אבינו'ס א דור שביעי, וואלט געהאט אזא הויך גרויסע נשמה און אזעלכע זכות אבות וי ער האט, וואלט יענער זיכער געווען בעסער וי ער איז . . .

אין די תמונות האותיות וואס הקדוש ברוך הוא האט געגעבן בסיני, איז פאראן דרייערליי אותיות, אתוון רברבין, אתוון בינונין, און אתוון זעירין. די תורה איז געשריבן אין אתוון בינונים. די כוונה איז, אז דער אדם באדארף זיין צו א בינוני, און דורך תורה קומט מען צו מדריגת בינוני. אדם הראשון, וואס דורך הכרת מעלת עצמו איז דורכגעפאלן בחטא עץ הדעת, שטייט "אדם" מיט א אלף רבתי; משה רבינו, וואס

> דורך דער עבודה פון הכרת שפלות עצמו איז ער צוגעקומען צו דער
> העכסטער דרגא פון ענוה, שטייט "ויקרא" מיט אן אלף זעירא.

The Previous Rebbe, [Rabbi Yosef Yitzchak Schneersohn,] once described at a Pesach *farbrengen* how the Alter Rebbe brought his grandson the *Tzemach Tzedek* to school when the latter was a small boy. The Alter Rebbe instructed the teacher to begin studying the book of *Vayikra*. After his first lesson with his teacher, the young boy asked his grandfather, "Why is the *alef* of the word *Vayikra* small?"

The Alter Rebbe entered into a spiritual trance for a short while and said:

"Adam was G-d's literal handiwork, about whom G-d testified that he was wiser than the angels. Adam was aware of his own worth, and that eventually got to him, ultimately leading to his downfall with the sin of the Tree of Knowledge.

"Moses, our Teacher . . . he, too, was aware of his own worth, but not only did it not go to his head, the very opposite happened: it caused him to be extremely broken and humble, as he thought that if another Jew—not Amram's son and the seventh scion from Abraham—would have possessed a soul as lofty as his and a pedigree like his, that person would have certainly outdone him. . . .

"When G-d gave the letters at Mount Sinai, they came in three sizes: small, medium, and large. The Torah is written with medium-sized letters, conveying the message that a person ought to be a *benoni*, which he or she can achieve by studying Torah. Whereas Adam stumbled into sin by dint of his excessive sense of self-worth, the *alef* of his name appears in large typeset. Whereas, by contrast, Moses achieved the greatest levels of humility by focusing on his unworthiness, so the *alef* associated with him is small."

TEXT 6

RABBI YITZCHAK BEN YEHUDAH HALEVI, PAANEACH RAZA, VAYIKRA 1:1

> "ויקרא" אל"ף זעירא, לומר: שאף שקראו השם יתברך, ועשה לו כל
> הכבוד הזה, ונדבר עמו תדיר – אף על פי כן, הקטין עצמו לפניו יתברך
> ולפני ישראל. ואל"ף של "אדם שת הבל" רבתי, לומר: שלא היה אדם
> גדול כמותו (כי נודע, שאף שאחר שמיעטו השם יתברך, העמידו על
> ק' אמה, או על רוב חכמה שהיה בו עד שקרא שמות).

Rabbi Yitzchak ben Yehudah Halevi
c. 1300

Bible commentator. Rabbi Yitzchak lived in France in the late 13th century and was a member of the French Tosafist school of biblical and Talmudic interpretation. He is known for his commentary on the Torah *Paaneach Raza*, which incorporates the teachings of earlier French and German scholars.

There is a small *alef* in the word *Vayikra* to teach us that, though G-d personally called him and afforded him all this honor to constantly speak with him, Moses nevertheless was always humble before G-d and the Jewish people. The *alef* of Adam's name is big to teach us that there was no greater person—either in a physical sense, for he was exceedingly tall, or in the sense of his superior wisdom, which he demonstrated when he gave names to all the animals.

TEXT 7

RABBI SHNEUR ZALMAN OF LIADI, LIKUTEI TORAH, VAYIKRA, 1B

> ובדברי הימים נאמר "אדם" באל"ף מאתוון רברבן, והוא בחינת אדם
> הראשון כמו שהיה לפני החטא, שהיה במדרגה גבוה מאד נעלה.

Rabbi Shneur Zalman of Liadi (Alter Rebbe)
1745–1812

Chasidic rebbe, halachic authority, and founder of the Chabad movement. The Alter Rebbe was born in Liozna, Belarus, and was among the principal students of the Magid of Mezeritch. His numerous works include the *Tanya*, an early classic containing the fundamentals of Chabad Chasidism; and *Shulchan Aruch HaRav,* an expanded and reworked code of Jewish law.

In Chronicles, Adam's name is written with a large *alef*, a reference to Adam's stature prior to the sin with the Tree of Knowledge. At that point, he was at an extremely lofty level.

III. COURAGEOUS HUMILITY

Be Like Adam!

TEXT 8

RABBI YOSEF YITZCHAK SCHNEERSOHN, LIKUTEI DIBURIM 4, P. 581A

מען דארף וויסען ווי אויסצונוצען די מעלות וואס יעדער האט.
אזוי ווי מען דארף וויסען די חסרונות, אזוי דארף מען וויסען די
אייגענע מעלות.

Everyone should learn how to utilize their own positive qualities. Just as one ought to know his or her own shortcomings, so
too should he or she know the positive qualities they possess.

**Rabbi Yosef Yitzchak
Schneersohn
(Rayatz, Frierdiker Rebbe,
Previous Rebbe)
1880–1950**

Chasidic rebbe, prolific writer, and Jewish
activist. Rabbi Yosef Yitzchak, the 6th
leader of the Chabad movement, actively
promoted Jewish religious practice in
Soviet Russia and was arrested for these
activities. After his release from prison
and exile, he settled in Warsaw, Poland,
from where he fled Nazi occupation and
arrived in New York in 1940. Settling in
Brooklyn, Rabbi Schneersohn worked
to revitalize American Jewish life. His
son-in-law, Rabbi Menachem Mendel
Schneerson, succeeded him as the
leader of the Chabad movement.

TEXT 9

THE REBBE, RABBI MENACHEM MENDEL SCHNEERSON, LIKUTEI SICHOT 17, P. 6

מצד דעם עילוי וואס איז דא ביי יעדער אידן, קען זיין ביי אים די
"הכרת מעלת עצמו", ווארום די מציאות פון א צדיק איז ניט קיין
אייגענע חס ושלום, נאר א מציאות דקדושה, אין וועלכער ס'איז ניטא
קיין אחיזה צו לעומת זה . . .

ואדרבא – עס דארף זיין הכרת מעלת עצמו, ביז אז לפעמים איז דאס
דער וועג (דורך "ויגבה לבו בדרכי ה'") ווי אזוי צו בייקומען די העלמות
והסתרים פון עולם הזה – זיין עבודה איז מיט א תוקף דקדושה,
בדוגמא צו עבודת הצדיקים.

Every Jew possesses tremendous worth, and, as such, any Jew can readily see his or her "self-worth." After all, a devout Jew's true value flows from a holy and G-dly source, and as such there is no concern that such thoughts (of self-worth) would ever lead to negative consequences.

What's more—a person *must* have this sense of self-worth, so much so that at times it is the only way to overcome the challenges of the mundane and material reality around us. When a Jew approaches his or her life with a proud and strong stance that flows from holiness akin to a *tzadik*, [all challenges dissipate].

Be Like Moses!

TEXT **10**

THE REBBE, RABBI MENACHEM MENDEL SCHNEERSON, LIKUTEI SICHOT 17, PP. 7–8

מען דארף באוואָרענען, אז שטייענדיק אין א תנועה פון תוקף
דקדושה והכרת מעלת עצמו, זאל זיך אין דעם ניט אריינמישן קיין
ישות כו' – איז ניט גענוג אז עס זאל זיין הכרת שפלות עצמו,
נאר עס מוז זיין אין דעם קצה ההפכי – ענווה וביטול בתכלית ...

און אויך אין דעם באשטייט גודל הענווה פון משה רבינו, וואָס האָט
מתקן געווען דעם חטא עץ הדעת [כידוע אז ביי מתן תורה – ווען
"משה קבל תורה מסיני" – איז "פסקה זוהמתן" פון חטא עץ הדעת].
ער איז געווען (ניט סתם אן עניו, נאר דער קצה ההפכי פון מציאות –)
"עניו מאד מכל האדם אשר על פני האדמה", ער האָט זיך פאַרמאָסטן
מיט יעדן איד, טראַכטנדיק, אז "יענער וואלט געהאט זיינע ... מעלות
... וואלט יענער זיכער זיין בעסער פאר אים".

While in a state of "holy pride" and being cognizant of our own
self-worth, we must be vigilant that our personal egos never get
involved. Not only must we be aware of our own shortcomings,
we must go to the *opposite extreme*—a radical sense of humility

and selflessness. . . .

It is here that we see Moses's tremendous humility—so much
so that it served as the antidote to the sin of the Tree of Knowledge [according to tradition, the "stain" of the primeval sin was
removed at *Matan Torah* when Moses received the Torah at
Mount Sinai]. Moses wasn't just a humble person; he was "*the
most humble man on the face of the earth.*" He would measure
himself up against every other person and conclude that "If
that person would have had my qualities, he or she would have
certainly surpassed me."

Conclusion

TEXT 11

TALMUD TRACTATE YEVAMOT, 61A

> "ואתן צאני, צאן מרעיתי, אדם אתם" – אתם קרויין אדם.

"And you, My sheep, the sheep of My pasture, are Adam"—you, the Jewish people, are called Adam.

TEXT 12

RABBI SHNEUR ZALMAN OF LIADI, TANYA, IGERET HAKODESH, CH. 7

> כל הנשמות שבעולם היו כלולות באדם הראשון. ודרך כלל – היתה נשמתו נחלקת למספר תרי"ג: רמ"ח אברים ושס"ה גידים. אך דרך פרט – נחלקת לניצוצות אין מספר, שהן נשמות כל ישראל מימות האבות והשבטים עד ביאת המשיח, ועד בכלל.

Every soul that has ever lived on earth was once part of Adam Harishon. Generally speaking, Adam's soul splits into 613 strains, but more specifically, it splits into innumerable sparks—which are the souls of every Jew from the beginning of time until the end of days.

Babylonian Talmud

A literary work of monumental proportions that draws upon the legal, spiritual, intellectual, ethical, and historical traditions of Judaism. The 37 tractates of the Babylonian Talmud contain the teachings of the Jewish sages from the period after the destruction of the 2nd Temple through the 5th century CE. It has served as the primary vehicle for the transmission of the Oral Law and the education of Jews over the centuries; it is the entry point for all subsequent legal, ethical, and theological Jewish scholarship.

Naming Powers from Adam

TEXT **13**

RABBI SHNEUR ZALMAN OF LIADI, TANYA, CH. 42

> כי כל נפש ונפש מבית ישראל יש בה מבחינת משה רבינו עליו השלום,
> כי הוא משבעה רועים הממשיכים חיות ואלוקות לכללות נשמות
> ישראל, שלכן נקראים בשם רועים. ומשה רבינו עליו השלום הוא
> כללות כולם, ונקרא "רעיא מהימנא".

Every Jewish soul possesses a dimension of Moses, for he was one of the "seven shepherds" who transmitted G-dly energy to the umbrella of the Jewish soul, which is the very reason they are called "shepherds." Moses was the ultimate shepherd, called the "faithful shepherd" in the *Zohar*.

12.

Pesach

The Freedom to Be You

Breaking Free from the Confusion of Egypt to the Clarity of Purpose

Dedicated to Rabbi Zalman and Hindel Levitin of Chabad of Palm Beach Island, Florida in recognition of their support and partnership with JLI in bringing Torah Studies to small communities across the globe

HOLIDAY OVERVIEW

Pesach

What Is Passover?

The eight-day festival of Passover is celebrated in the early spring, from the 15th through the 22nd of the Hebrew month of Nisan. It commemorates the emancipation of the Israelites from slavery in ancient Egypt. And, by following the rituals of Passover, we have the ability to relive and experience the true freedom that our ancestors gained.

The Story in a Nutshell

After many decades of slavery to the Egyptian pharaohs, during which time the Israelites were subjected to backbreaking labor and unbearable horrors, G-d saw the people's distress and sent Moses to Pharaoh with a message: "Send forth My people, so that they may serve Me." But despite numerous warnings, Pharaoh refused to heed G-d's command. G-d then sent upon Egypt ten devastating plagues, afflicting them and destroying everything from their livestock to their crops.

At the stroke of midnight of 15 Nisan in the year 2448 from Creation (1313 BCE), G-d visited the last of the ten plagues on the Egyptians, killing all their firstborns. While doing so, G-d spared the Children of Israel, "passing over" their homes—hence the name of the holiday. Pharaoh's resistance was broken, and he virtually chased his former slaves out of the land. The Israelites left in such a hurry, in fact, that the bread they baked as provisions for the way did not have time to rise. Six hundred thousand adult males, plus many more women and children, left Egypt on that day, and began the trek to Mount Sinai and their birth as G-d's chosen people.

Passover Observances

Passover is divided into two parts:

The first two days and last two days (the latter commemorating the Splitting of the Red Sea) are full-fledged holidays. Holiday candles are lit at night, and *kiddush* and sumptuous holiday meals are enjoyed on both nights and days. We don't go to work, drive, write, or switch on or off electric devices. We are permitted to cook and to carry outdoors.

The middle four days are called *chol hamoed*, semi-festive "intermediate days," when most forms of work are permitted.

To commemorate the unleavened bread that the Israelites ate when they left Egypt, we don't eat—or even retain in our possession—any *chametz* from midday of the day before Passover until the conclusion of the holiday. *Chametz* means leavened grain—any food or drink that contains even a trace of wheat, barley, rye, oats, spelt, or their derivatives, and which wasn't guarded from leavening or fermentation. This includes bread, cake, cookies, cereal, pasta, and most alcoholic beverages. Moreover, almost any processed food or drink can be assumed to be *chametz* unless certified otherwise.

Ridding our homes of *chametz* is an intensive process. It involves a full-out spring-cleaning search-and-destroy mission during the weeks before Passover, and culminates with a ceremonial search for *chametz* on the night before Passover, and then a *chametz*-burning ceremony on the morning before the holiday. *Chametz* that cannot be disposed of can be sold to a non-Jew for the duration of the holiday.

Instead of *chametz*, we eat matzah—flat unleavened bread. It is a mitzvah to partake of matzah on the two *seder* nights (see below for more on this), and during the rest of the holiday (except Shabbat) it is optional.

The highlight of Passover is the *seder*, observed on each of the first two nights of the holiday. The *seder* is a fifteen-step family-oriented tradition and ritual-packed feast.

I. BIRTH OF A PEOPLE

The Day You Were Born

TEXT 1

YECHEZKEL (EZEKIEL) 16:4–10

וּמוֹלְדוֹתַיִךְ בְּיוֹם הוּלֶּדֶת אֹתָךְ, לֹא כָרַת שָׁרֵּךְ וּבְמַיִם לֹא רֻחַצְתְּ לְמִשְׁעִי, וְהָמְלֵחַ לֹא הֻמְלַחַתְּ וְהָחְתֵּל לֹא חֻתָּלְתְּ:

לֹא חָסָה עָלַיִךְ עַיִן לַעֲשׂוֹת לָךְ אַחַת מֵאֵלֶּה לְחֻמְלָה עָלָיִךְ, וַתֻּשְׁלְכִי אֶל פְּנֵי הַשָּׂדֶה בְּגֹעַל נַפְשֵׁךְ בְּיוֹם הֻלֶּדֶת אֹתָךְ:

וָאֶעֱבֹר עָלַיִךְ וָאֶרְאֵךְ מִתְבּוֹסֶסֶת בְּדָמָיִךְ, וָאֹמַר לָךְ בְּדָמַיִךְ חֲיִי, וָאֹמַר לָךְ בְּדָמַיִךְ חֲיִי:

רְבָבָה כְּצֶמַח הַשָּׂדֶה נְתַתִּיךְ, וַתִּרְבִּי וַתִּגְדְּלִי וַתָּבֹאִי בַּעֲדִי עֲדָיִים, שָׁדַיִם נָכֹנוּ וּשְׂעָרֵךְ צִמֵּחַ, וְאַתְּ עֵרֹם וְעֶרְיָה:

וָאֶעֱבֹר עָלַיִךְ וָאֶרְאֵךְ וְהִנֵּה עִתֵּךְ עֵת דֹּדִים, וָאֶפְרֹשׂ כְּנָפִי עָלַיִךְ וָאֲכַסֶּה עֶרְוָתֵךְ, וָאֶשָּׁבַע לָךְ וָאָבוֹא בִבְרִית אֹתָךְ, נְאֻם ה' אֱלֹקִים וַתִּהְיִי לִי:

וָאֶרְחָצֵךְ בַּמַּיִם וָאֶשְׁטֹף דָּמַיִךְ מֵעָלָיִךְ, וָאֲסֻכֵךְ בַּשָּׁמֶן:

וָאַלְבִּישֵׁךְ רִקְמָה וָאֶנְעֲלֵךְ תָּחַשׁ, וָאֶחְבְּשֵׁךְ בַּשֵּׁשׁ וַאֲכַסֵּךְ מֶשִׁי:

"And as for your birth, on the day you were born, your navel was not cut, neither were you washed with water for cleansing, nor were you salted, nor swaddled at all.

"No eye pitied you [enough] to do for you any of those, to have mercy on you, and you were cast on the open field in the loathsomeness of your body on the day you were born.

"And I passed by you and saw you downtrodden with your blood, and I said to you, 'With your blood, live,' and I said to you, 'With your blood, live.'

"Myriads, like the plants of the field, I have made you, and you have increased and grown, and you have come with perfect beauty, breasts fashioned and your hair grown, but you were naked and bare.

"And I passed by you and saw you, and behold, your time was the time of love, and I spread My skirt over you, and I covered your nakedness, and I swore to you and came into a covenant with you," says the L-rd, "and you were Mine.

"And I washed you with water, and I rinsed your blood off you, and I anointed you with oil.

"And I clothed you with embroidered garments, and I shod you with [the skin of the] badger, and I girded you with fine linen, and I covered you with silk."

TEXT **2**

RASHI, AD LOC.

> "ביום הולדת אותך": כשבחרתי בך במצרים היית בלי שום תיקון. ולפי שדימה הדבר ללידה, הזכיר כאן תיקוני הולד.

Rabbi Shlomo Yitzchaki (Rashi)
1040–1105

Most noted biblical and Talmudic commentator. Born in Troyes, France, Rashi studied in the famed *yeshivot* of Mainz and Worms. His commentaries on the Pentateuch and the Talmud, which focus on the straightforward meaning of the text, appear in virtually every edition of the Talmud and Bible.

"On the day you were born." When I chose you in Egypt, you were entirely bare. Because the Exodus is compared to birth, the verses relate the various stages of caring for a newborn.

A Nation Enslaved

TEXT 3

DEVARIM (DEUTERONOMY) 26:5–9

וְעָנִיתָ וְאָמַרְתָּ לִפְנֵי ה' אֱלֹקֶיךָ, אֲרַמִּי אֹבֵד אָבִי, וַיֵּרֶד מִצְרַיְמָה וַיָּגָר שָׁם בִּמְתֵי מְעָט, וַיְהִי שָׁם לְגוֹי גָּדוֹל עָצוּם וָרָב:

וַיָּרֵעוּ אֹתָנוּ הַמִּצְרִים וַיְעַנּוּנוּ, וַיִּתְּנוּ עָלֵינוּ עֲבֹדָה קָשָׁה:

וַנִּצְעַק אֶל ה' אֱלֹקֵי אֲבֹתֵינוּ, וַיִּשְׁמַע ה' אֶת קֹלֵנוּ, וַיַּרְא אֶת עָנְיֵנוּ וְאֶת עֲמָלֵנוּ וְאֶת לַחֲצֵנוּ:

וַיּוֹצִאֵנוּ ה' מִמִּצְרַיִם, בְּיָד חֲזָקָה וּבִזְרֹעַ נְטוּיָה וּבְמֹרָא גָּדֹל, וּבְאֹתוֹת וּבְמֹפְתִים:

וַיְבִאֵנוּ אֶל הַמָּקוֹם הַזֶּה, וַיִּתֶּן לָנוּ אֶת הָאָרֶץ הַזֹּאת, אֶרֶץ זָבַת חָלָב וּדְבָשׁ:

And you shall call out and say before the L-rd, your G-d, "An Aramean [sought to] destroy my forefather, and he went down to Egypt and sojourned there with a small number of people, and there, he became a great, mighty, and numerous nation.

"And the Egyptians treated us cruelly and afflicted us, and they imposed hard labor upon us.

"So we cried out to the L-rd, G-d of our fathers, and the L-rd heard our voice and saw our affliction, our toil, and our oppression.

"And G-d brought us out from Egypt with a strong hand and with an outstretched arm, with great awe, and with signs and wonders.

"And He brought us to this place, and He gave us this land, a land flowing with milk and honey."

"A New Entity"

TEXT 4

THE REBBE, RABBI MENACHEM MENDEL SCHNEERSON, LIKUTEI SICHOT 17, P. 71

> דער זמן פון יציאת מצרים איז – כמבואר בנבואת יחזקאל – לידת עם
> ישראל. דער טעם וואס מ'איז עס מתאר מיטן לשון "לידה", איז . . .
> ווייל ווערנדיק א פאלק זיינען אידן דורכדעם פארוואנדלט געווארן אין
> א "מציאות חדשה".

The Exodus is referred to in Ezekiel's prophecy as the "birth" of the Jewish people. The reason it is called a "birth" is because . . . the Jewish people became a "new entity."

Rabbi Menachem Mendel Schneerson
1902–1994

The towering Jewish leader of the 20th century, known as "the Lubavitcher Rebbe," or simply as "the Rebbe." Born in southern Ukraine, the Rebbe escaped Nazi-occupied Europe, arriving in the U.S. in June 1941. The Rebbe inspired and guided the revival of traditional Judaism after the European devastation, impacting virtually every Jewish community the world over. The Rebbe often emphasized that the performance of just one additional good deed could usher in the era of Mashiach. The Rebbe's scholarly talks and writings have been printed in more than 200 volumes.

II. THE WORK OF FREEDOM

Moses Leaves Town

TEXT 5a

SHEMOT (EXODUS) 9:25–29

> וַיַּךְ הַבָּרָד בְּכָל אֶרֶץ מִצְרַיִם, אֵת כָּל אֲשֶׁר בַּשָּׂדֶה, מֵאָדָם וְעַד בְּהֵמָה. וְאֵת
> כָּל עֵשֶׂב הַשָּׂדֶה הִכָּה הַבָּרָד, וְאֶת כָּל עֵץ הַשָּׂדֶה שִׁבֵּר:
>
> רַק בְּאֶרֶץ גֹּשֶׁן, אֲשֶׁר שָׁם בְּנֵי יִשְׂרָאֵל, לֹא הָיָה בָּרָד:
>
> וַיִּשְׁלַח פַּרְעֹה וַיִּקְרָא לְמֹשֶׁה וּלְאַהֲרֹן, וַיֹּאמֶר אֲלֵהֶם חָטָאתִי הַפָּעַם, ה'
> הַצַּדִּיק וַאֲנִי וְעַמִּי הָרְשָׁעִים:
>
> הַעְתִּירוּ אֶל ה' וְרַב מִהְיֹת קֹלֹת אֱלֹקִים וּבָרָד, וַאֲשַׁלְּחָה אֶתְכֶם, וְלֹא
> תֹסִפוּן לַעֲמֹד:
>
> וַיֹּאמֶר אֵלָיו מֹשֶׁה, כְּצֵאתִי אֶת הָעִיר אֶפְרֹשׂ אֶת כַּפַּי אֶל ה', הַקֹּלוֹת
> יֶחְדָּלוּן וְהַבָּרָד לֹא יִהְיֶה עוֹד, לְמַעַן תֵּדַע כִּי לה' הָאָרֶץ:

The hail struck throughout the entire land of Egypt—all that was in the field, both man and beast—and the hail struck all the vegetation of the field, and it broke all the trees of the field.

Only in the land of Goshen, where the Children of Israel were, there was no hail.

So Pharaoh sent and summoned Moses and Aaron and said to them, "I have sinned this time. G-d is the righteous One, and I and my people are the guilty ones.

"Entreat G-d, and let it be enough of G-d's thunder and hail, and I will let you go, and you shall not continue to stand."

And Moses said to him, "When I leave the city, I will spread my hands to G-d. The thunder will cease, and there will be no more hail, in order that you know that the land is G-d's."

TEXT 5b

RASHI, AD LOC.

"כצאתי את העיר": מן העיה, אבל בתוך העיר לא התפלל, לפי שהיתה
מלאה גילולים.

"When l leave the city." But within the city he did not pray, because it was full of idols.

Steeped in Evil

TEXT 6

THE REBBE, RABBI MENACHEM MENDEL SCHNEERSON, TORAT
MENACHEM HITVAADUYOT 5721:2, PP. 214–215

עצם הענין דעבודה זרה – הרי בכל כדור הארץ ישנה האפשריות לזה,
ועד שבכמה מקומות ישנה (לא רק האפשריות, אלא) גם המציאות
דעבודה זרה, אבל אף על פי כן, אין זה באופן ד"מלאה גילולים", כי יש
שם גם עוד ענינים מלבד עבודה זרה; מה שאין כן ארץ מצרים היתה
"מלאה גילולים", דהיינו, שכל ענין איזה שיהיה ("וואָס מען זאָל נאָר
ניט אָנכאַפּן"), היה מלא בעבודה זרה.

והיינו, שכשם שבקדושה, להבדיל, צריך להיות "בכל דרכיך דעהו",
דהיינו שבכל הענינים, אכילה ושתיה וכו', צריך להיות הדעת
והתקשרות עם אלקות – כמו כן היה במצרים לאידך גיסא, ש"בכל
דרכיך" היתה "מלאה גילולים".

Idolatry can exist anywhere in the world. In some places, (it not only can exist, but) it in fact does exist. Nevertheless, a given place is not usually "full of idolatry"; things other than idolatry exist there as well. But the land of Egypt was "full of idolatry," meaning anything there, whatever it may have been, was full of idolatry.

In other words: Just like in the realm of holiness, *lehavdil*, one must "know G-d in all your ways"—meaning one must connect everything one eats, drinks, etc., with G-dliness—in Egypt it was just the opposite. In "all their ways"—everything was "full of idolatry."

Backbreaking, Soul Crushing

TEXT 7a

SHEMOT (EXODUS) 1:13–14

וַיַּעֲבִדוּ מִצְרַיִם אֶת בְּנֵי יִשְׂרָאֵל בְּפָרֶךְ:

וַיְמָרֲרוּ אֶת חַיֵּיהֶם בַּעֲבֹדָה קָשָׁה, בְּחֹמֶר וּבִלְבֵנִים וּבְכָל עֲבֹדָה בַּשָּׂדֶה, אֵת כָּל עֲבֹדָתָם אֲשֶׁר עָבְדוּ בָהֶם בְּפָרֶךְ:

So the Egyptians enslaved the Children of Israel with backbreaking labor.

And they embittered their lives with hard labor, with clay and with bricks and with all kinds of labor in the fields, all their work that they worked with them with backbreaking labor.

TEXT 7b

TALMUD TRACTATE SOTAH, 11B

"את כל עבודתם אשר עבדו בהם בפרך": אמר רבי שמואל בר נחמני, אמר רבי יונתן: שהיו מחליפין מלאכת אנשים לנשים, ומלאכת נשים לאנשים.

Babylonian Talmud

A literary work of monumental proportions that draws upon the legal, spiritual, intellectual, ethical, and historical traditions of Judaism. The 37 tractates of the Babylonian Talmud contain the teachings of the Jewish sages from the period after the destruction of the 2nd Temple through the 5th century CE. It has served as the primary vehicle for the transmission of the Oral Law and the education of Jews over the centuries; it is the entry point for all subsequent legal, ethical, and theological Jewish scholarship.

"All their work that they worked with them with backbreaking labor." Rabbi Shmuel bar Nachmani said in the name of Rabbi Yonatan, "This means they would exchange the responsibilities of men and women, giving men's work to women and women's work to men [requiring everyone to do work to which they were unaccustomed]."

You Need to Be You

TEXT **8**

SHEMOT (EXODUS) 3:11–12

וַיֹּאמֶר מֹשֶׁה אֶל הָאֱלֹקִים, מִי אָנֹכִי כִּי אֵלֵךְ אֶל פַּרְעֹה וְכִי אוֹצִיא אֶת בְּנֵי
יִשְׂרָאֵל מִמִּצְרָיִם:

וַיֹּאמֶר, כִּי אֶהְיֶה עִמָּךְ, וְזֶה לְךָ הָאוֹת כִּי אָנֹכִי שְׁלַחְתִּיךָ, בְּהוֹצִיאֲךָ אֶת הָעָם
מִמִּצְרַיִם, תַּעַבְדוּן אֶת הָאֱלֹקִים עַל הָהָר הַזֶּה:

But Moses said to G-d, "Who am I that I should go to Pharaoh, and that I should take the Children of Israel out of Egypt?"

And He said, "For I will be with you, and this is the sign for you that it was I Who sent you. When you take the people out of Egypt, you will worship G-d on this mountain."

How to Be Free

TEXT **9**

PIRKEI AVOT (ETHICS OF THE FATHERS) 6:2

אָמַר רַבִּי יְהוֹשֻׁעַ בֶּן לֵוִי . . . "וְהַלֻּחֹת מַעֲשֵׂה אֱלֹקִים הֵמָּה, וְהַמִּכְתָּב
מִכְתַּב אֱלֹקִים הוּא, חָרוּת עַל הַלֻּחֹת", אַל תִּקְרֵי חָרוּת אֶלָּא חֵרוּת, שֶׁאֵין
לְךָ בֶּן חוֹרִין, אֶלָּא מִי שֶׁעוֹסֵק בְּתַלְמוּד תּוֹרָה.

Rabbi Yehoshua the son of Levi said . . . "The verse states, 'And the Tablets are the work of G-d, and the writing is G-d's writing, engraved in the Tablets.' Read not 'engraved' (*charut*) but 'liberty' (*cheirut*)—for there is no free individual except for one who occupies themselves with Torah study."

> **Ethics of the Fathers (*Pirkei Avot*)**
>
> A 6-chapter work on Jewish ethics that is studied widely by Jewish communities, especially during the summer. The first 5 chapters are from the Mishnah, tractate Avot. Avot differs from the rest of the Mishnah in that it does not focus on legal subjects; it is a collection of the sages' wisdom on topics related to character development, ethics, healthy living, piety, and the study of Torah.

TEXT 10

THE REBBE, RABBI MENACHEM MENDEL SCHNEERSON, LIKUTEI SICHOT 17, P. 75

ווען א איד איז ניט מקיים תורה ומצוות רחמנא ליצלן, איז כאטש אז
אים זעט אויס אז ער איז "פריי" אן א יאך, און אז ס'איז אים אזוי
גרינגער ווי ווען ער וואלט יא מקיים געווען תומ"צ – וויבאלד אבער
אז דאס (פירן א לעבן ניט על פי תורה, חס ושלום) איז היפך ווי עס
פאדערט זיין אמת'ער מהות וטבע, איז עס אן ענין פון "עבודת פרך"...
דוקא ווען עס איז דא דער "תעבדון", איז ער אן אמת'ער בן חורין.

One who neglects the Torah and *mitzvot* might appear "liberated," without a yoke upon him. It seems like an easier way to live than keeping the Torah and *mitzvot*. But because this (neglecting the Torah, G-d forbid) runs contrary to a Jew's very identity, ultimately, it is a form of "backbreaking labor." . . . Only when one "serves" G-d can they truly be free.

The Shavuot Connection

TEXT 11

THE REBBE, RABBI MENACHEM MENDEL SCHNEERSON, IBID., PP. 71–72

דער תכלית און כוונה (און שלימות) פון יציאת מצרים איז מתן תורה,
כמו שנאמר: "בהוציאך את העם ממצרים, תעבדון את האלקים על
ההר הזה".

[וואס דאס איז איינער פון די ביאורים פארוואס חג השבועות – זמן
מתן תורתנו – ווערט באשטימט דורך (ציילן שבע שבתות פון מחרת
ה)פסח, להורות אז שבועות (מתן תורה) איז א המשך פון יציאת
מצרים, לידת עם ישראל].

The purpose (and completion) of the Exodus is receiving the
Torah at Mount Sinai, as the verse states, "When you take the
people out of Egypt, you will worship G-d on this mountain."

III. LIVING THE LIFE

A Nation Born Anew

TEXT 12

THE REBBE, RABBI MENACHEM MENDEL SCHNEERSON, IBID., P. 72

דאס הייסט, לידת עם ישראל איז פארבונדן מיט דעם וואס זיי ווערן
א תורה פאלק – דער גאנצער מהות פון אידן (אויך אלס א יחיד)
איז תורה.

[און די מציאות חדשה איז ניט נאר דערפאר וואס אין גלות מצרים
זיינען אידן געווען אין א שפל המצב ביותר, און זיינען במילא מצד
עצמם ניט געווען קיין כלים אויפצונעמען תורה – ואדרבה: זייענדיק
אין מ"ט שערי טומאה איז זייער מצב געווען בניגוד צו תורה (וקדושה):

נאר בעיקר מצד דעם וואס תורה איז "אצלו אמון גו' שעשועים",
חמדה גנוזה שגנוזה לך – זי איז איינגאנצן העכער פון נבראים, און
דעריבער איז עס בײ אידן (ווי זיי זיינען למטה, און דערצו נאך – אין
מצרים) געווען א דבר חדש לגמרי, עס איז ניט אין זייער גדר].

The birth of the Jewish people is about becoming a Torah
nation—i.e., the whole identity of Jews [and of each individual
Jew] is Torah.

(The reason there is a new identity is not just because in Egypt
they were at such a lowly spiritual place that they weren't able
to appreciate the Torah, and, in fact, as long as they were in
the forty-nine gates of impurity [in Egypt], their spiritual state
opposed Torah [and holiness].

Rather, it is mainly because Torah is "A nursling beside Him,
and I was [His] delight every day," and a "Hidden treasure that
was concealed by You." It completely transcends the created
realm, and therefore it was something entirely new for the Jewish people [when they were in Egypt]—completely out of their
former league.)

Conversion and Birth

TEXT 13

TALMUD TRACTATE YEVAMOT, 22A

> וגר שנתגייר, כקטן שנולד דמי.

A convert who converts is like a newborn baby.

TEXT 14

RABBI YOSEF YITZCHAK SCHNEERSOHN, IGROT KODESH 8, P. 208

> אויף דעם האט . . . מורנו הבעל שם טוב נשמתו עדן געזאגט . . . א
> איד האט זיך קיינמאל ניט געשמדט, און א גוי האט זיך קיינמאל ניט
> מגייר געווען . . . דער וואס האט זיך מגייר געווען איז לכתחילה געווען
> א איד, ער האט געהאט די יחידה שבנפש.

Rabbi Yosef Yitzchak Schneersohn (Rayatz, Frierdiker Rebbe, Previous Rebbe) 1880–1950

Chasidic rebbe, prolific writer, and Jewish activist. Rabbi Yosef Yitschak, the sixth leader of the Chabad movement, actively promoted Jewish religious practice in Soviet Russia and was arrested for these activities. After his release from prison and exile, he settled in Warsaw, Poland, from where he fled Nazi occupation and arrived in New York in 1940. Settling in Brooklyn, Rabbi Schneersohn worked to revitalize American Jewish life. His son-in-law Rabbi Menachem Mendel Schneerson succeeded him as the leader of the Chabad movement.

Our master the Baal Shem Tov said . . . "A Jew can never shed his Judaism, and a gentile can never convert. . . . One who converts was always Jewish, always possessed the spark of a Jewish soul."

A Chasid's "Birthday"

TEXT 15

THE REBBE, RABBI MENACHEM MENDEL SCHNEERSON, HAYOM YOM, 30 SHEVAT

כמה וכמה חסידים חשבו יום בואם לליובאוויטש ליום הולדת שלהם. מורי הרב שמואל בצלאל בא בפעם הראשונה לליובאוויטש אור ליום ששי פרשת משפטים שנת תר"ח, ובכל שנה ושנה היה ער כל אותו הלילה, ומכוון להניח תפילין בה בשעה אשר נכנס להצמח צדק בפעם הראשונה.

Hayom Yom

In 1942, Rabbi Yosef Yitzchak Schneersohn, the 6th Rebbe of Chabad, gave his son-in-law, the future Rebbe, the task of compiling an anthology of Chasidic aphorisms and customs arranged according to the days of the year. In describing the completed product, Rabbi Yosef Yitzchak wrote that it is "a book that is small in format but bursting with pearls and diamonds of the choicest quality."

Many Chasidim considered the day they arrived in Lubavitch to be their "birthday." My teacher, Rabbi Shmuel Betzalel, arrived in Lubavitch for the first time on Thursday evening, *Parshat Mishpatim* 5608 (1848). Every year after that, he stayed awake all that night and took pains to put on his *tefilin* at the exact time he had entered the *Tzemach Tzedek's* chamber for *yechidus* the first time.

THE ROHR
Jewish Learning Institute

832 Eastern Parkway, Brooklyn, New York 11213

CHAIRMAN
Rabbi Moshe Kotlarsky
Lubavitch World Headquarters,
New York, NY

PRINCIPAL BENEFACTOR
Mr. George Rohr
New York, NY

EXECUTIVE DIRECTOR
Rabbi Efraim Mintz

ADMINISTRATION
Rabbi Mendel Kotlarsky

ADMINISTRATOR
Rabbi Dubi Rabinowitz

EXECUTIVE COMMITTEE
Rabbi Chaim Block
S. Antonio, TX
Rabbi Hesh Epstein
Columbia, SC
Rabbi Ronnie Fine
Montreal, Quebec
Rabbi Yosef Gansburg
Toronto, Ontario
Rabbi Shmuel Kaplan
Potomac, MD
Rabbi Yisrael Rice
S. Rafael, CA
Rabbi Avrohom Sternberg
New London, CT

TORAH STUDIES

CHAIRMAN
Rabbi Yosef Gansburg
Toronto, Ontario

MANAGING EDITOR
Rabbi Ahrele Loschak
Brooklyn, NY

ADMINISTRATOR
Rabbi Shlomie Tenenbaum
Brooklyn, NY

FOUNDING DIRECTOR
Rabbi Meir Hecht
Chicago, IL

STEERING COMMITTEE
Rabbi Levi Fogelman
Natick, MA
Rabbi Yaakov Halperin
Allentown, PA
Rabbi Nechemiah Schusterman
Peabody, MA
Rabbi Ari Sollish
Atlanta, GA

CONTENT EDITORS
Rabbi Eliezer Gurkow
London, ON
Rabbi Zalman Margolin
Miami, FL
Rabbi Yitzchok Schmukler
Brooklyn, NY
Rabbi Boruch Werdiger
Palm Springs, CA

MARKETING AND PR
Rabbi Zalman M. Abraham

PUBLICATION DESIGN
Mrs. Shayna Grosh
Rabbi Motti Klein
Rabbi Zalman Korf
Rabbi Moshe Wolff

GRAPHIC DESIGN
Mrs. Chaya Mushka Kanner
Ms. Chaya Mintz
Mrs. Mussi Sharfstein

PROOFREADING
Dr. Rakefet Orobona
Parker, CO
Ms. Mimi Palace
Brooklyn, NY
Mrs. Rachel Musicante
Silver Springs, MD
Mrs. Ya'akovah Weber
Brooklyn, NY

COPY EDITING
Mr. Michael Barnett
Bel Air, MD

POWERPOINT DESIGN
Mrs. Bunie Chazan
Manchester, England

PRODUCTION
Rabbi Mendel Sirota
Brooklyn, NY

An affiliate of
Merkos L'Inyonei Chinuch
The Educational Arm of the Worldwide Chabad-
Lubavitch Movement

JEWISH LEARNING INSTITUTE

The Jewish Learning Multiplex

Brought to you by the Rohr Jewish Learning Institute

In fulfillment of the mandate of the Lubavitcher Rebbe, of blessed memory, whose leadership guides every step of our work, the mission of the Rohr Jewish Learning Institute is to transform Jewish life and the greater community through the study of Torah, connecting each Jew to our shared heritage of Jewish learning.

While our flagship program remains the cornerstone of our organization, JLI is proud to feature additional divisions catering to specific populations, in order to meet a wide array of educational needs.

The Rohr JEWISH LEARNING INSTITUTE

a subsidiary of Merkos L'Inyonei Chinuch,
the adult educational arm of the Chabad-Lubavitch movement

TORAH STUDIES

Torah Studies provides a rich and nuanced
encounter with the weekly Torah reading.

MYSHIUR
TALMUD LEARNING INITIATIVE

MyShiur courses are designed to assist students in
developing the skills needed to study Talmud independently.

SINAI SCHOLARS SOCIETY

This rigorous fellowship program invites select college
students to explore the fundamentals of Judaism.

JLI TEENS
YOUNG SMART JEWISH

IN PARTNERSHIP WITH CTEEN: CHABAD TEEN NETWORK

Jewish teens forge their identity as they engage in
Torah study, social interaction, and serious fun.

ROSHCHODESH
society

The Rosh Chodesh Society gathers Jewish women
together once a month for intensive textual study.

TORAHCafé

TorahCafe.com provides an exclusive selection
of top-rated Jewish educational videos.

BRILLIANT LEARNING. NATURALLY.

NATIONAL JEWISH RETREAT

This yearly event rejuvenates mind, body, and spirit with
a powerful synthesis of Jewish learning and community.

THE LAND & THE SPIRIT
JLI ISRAEL EXPERIENCE

Participants delve into our nation's past while exploring
the Holy Land's relevance and meaning today.

JLI ACADEMY
PEDAGOGY · CURRICULUM · MENTORING

Select affiliates are invited to partner with peers and noted
professionals, as leaders of innovation and excellence.

THE SAMI ROHR RESEARCH INSTITUTE

Machon Shmuel is an institute providing Torah
research in the service of educators worldwide.

NOTES